BLACK BELT
B · O · O · K · S

T0149909

BEYOND
KUNG FU

Breaking an Opponent's Power Through Relaxed Tension

LEO T. FONG

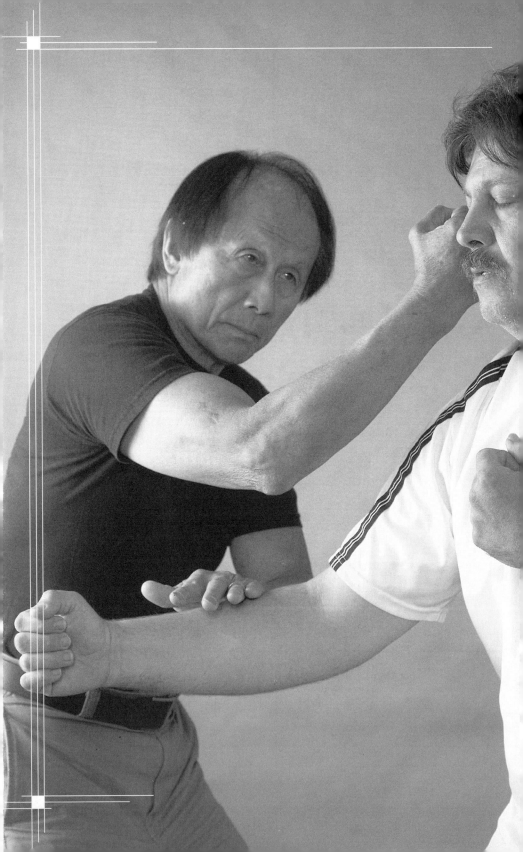

BEYOND KUNG FU

Breaking an Opponent's Power Through Relaxed Tension

LEO T. FONG

Edited by Sarah Dzida, Raymond Horwitz, Jeannine Santiago and Jon Sattler

Cover Design by Kobranto Creative

Graphic Design by John Bodine

Photography by Rick Hustead

Models: Barry Bostain and Adam James

©2009 Black Belt Communications LLC

All Rights Reserved
Printed in the United States of America

Library of Congress Control Number: 2009929492
ISBN-10: 0-89750-179-9
ISBN-13: 978-0-89750-179-8

First Printing 2009

WARNING

This book is presented only as a means of preserving a unique aspect of the heritage of the martial arts. Neither Ohara Publications nor the author make any representation, warranty or guarantee that the techniques described or illustrated in this book will be safe or effective in any self-defense situation or otherwise. You may be injured if you apply or train in the techniques illustrated in this book and neither Ohara Publications nor the author is responsible for any such injury that may result. It is essential that you consult a physician regarding whether or not to attempt any technique described in this book. Specific self-defense responses illustrated in this book may not be justified in any particular situation in view of all of the circumstances or under applicable federal, state or local law. Neither Ohara Publications nor the author make any representation or warranty regarding the legality or appropriateness of any technique mentioned in this book.

BLACK BELT BOOKS
A Division of **OHARA** 📖 **PUBLICATIONS, INC.**
World Leader in Martial Arts Publications

DEDICATION

To Minnie

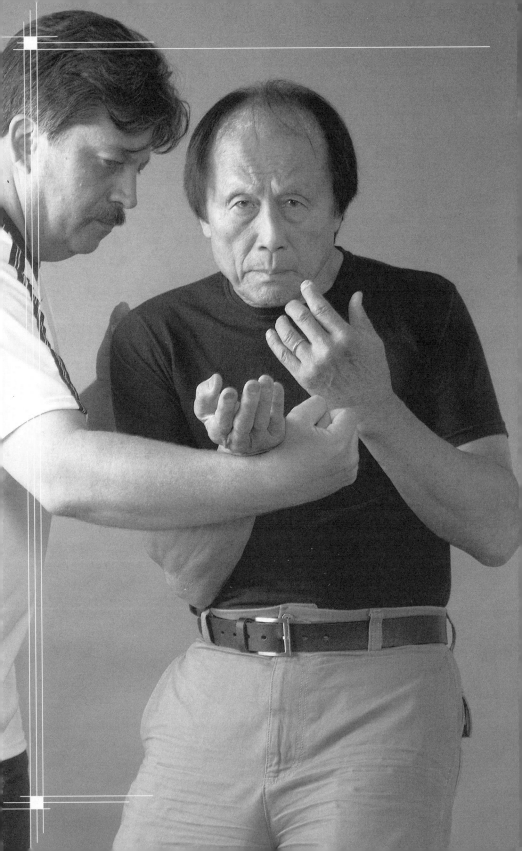

ACKNOWLEDGMENTS

A special thanks and appreciation to Adam James and Barry Bostain for posing for the pictures in this book.

To the Black Belt Communications staff and Sarah Dzida for making this project a reality.

And to Dr. Thomas J. Nardi, a friend of more than 35 years, for his precise and clear explanation in the Foreword of what this book is about.

ABOUT THE AUTHOR

by Adam James

Leo T. Fong was born in Guangdong (Canton) China on November 23, 1928, in the Year of the Dragon. He immigrated to the United States at age 5 with his mother to join his father in Widener, Arkansas, where his father operated a mom and pop grocery store.

The racist social environment of the mid-1930s defined for Fong the direction of his life. It was the reason his martial arts journey began: At age 7, one of his classmates said something racist and young Fong punched him in the face.

Unlike many of his Chinese cousins who refused to go back to school because of the teasing and bullying, Fong chose to fight rather than take flight. He began to take an interest in physical fitness, and at age 12, he purchased a book, *The Fundamentals of Boxing*, by world middleweight-boxing champion Barney Ross. Fong studied the book and practiced what he learned. His boxing skills enabled him to survive many street encounters without injuries.

At age 16, Fong had a religious experience during a lingering two-week sickness. He promised God that he would go into the ministry if he were healed from a lingering two-week sickness. This commitment led him to attend Hendrix College, a small United Methodist university in Conway, Arkansas. Hendrix happened to have boxing and wrestling programs. After sparring with and defeating several wrestlers, Fong chose to join the Hendrix boxing team. It was here that he took his first formal boxing lesson, which was taught by Kirby "KO" Donoho, a former boxing champion.

He continued his boxing career after he graduated from Hendrix College and entered Southern Methodist University in Dallas for his seminary training. In 1952 during his first year at SMU, Fong entered the Southwestern Amateur Athletic Union boxing championship and fought his way to the finals. The *Dallas Morning News* said that Fong "had ringsiders buzzing with his 15-second first-round knockout of his opponent Bill Morgan." After graduating from SMU, Fong was assigned to a church in Sacramento, California. In Sacramento, he began to take an interest in traditional martial arts such as *jujutsu*, judo, *taekwondo* and kung fu.

In 1962, he met Bruce Lee at James Yimm Lee's house. It was the beginning of a 10-year friendship. Over that period of time, Fong and Lee had many martial arts conversations, interactions and workouts together. After Lee's death, Fong continued his martial arts journey.

In 1974, Fong was offered a role in a feature film in the Philippines. It was there that he took an interest in the Philippine arts of *arnis* and *escrima*. He trained with two of the top instructors of the art: Remy Presas and Angel Cabales. When he returned to the United States, he decided to pursue a career in acting and became involved in dozens of movies and documentaries.

In 1972, he was approached by Mito Uyehara—the founder of *Black Belt* and Ohara Publications—to write a book on *sil lum* kung fu. This first endeavor led to a career in writing. Fong has since penned more than 25 martial arts and inspirational books. He has also written 10 movie scripts that were made into movies.

In 2006, *Black Belt* honored Fong by inducting him into the *Black Belt* Hall of Fame as its Kung Fu Artist of the Year. At age 80, Fong continues to live an active lifestyle. He travels frequently overseas and to the East Coast to conduct martial arts seminars. He trains two hours a day and teaches seven senior-exercise classes a week. On the weekends, he teaches privately at Warner Park in Woodlands, California.

Beyond Kung Fu: Breaking an Opponent's Power Through Relaxed Tension is a culmination of more than 70 years of research and practice in the martial arts. This book is a testimony that the journey begins with the physical and evolves toward the spiritual.

FOREWORD

THE PSYCHOLOGY OF YIELDING (RELAXED TENSION)

by Dr. Thomas J. Nardi

What comes to mind when you hear the word "yield"? To the Western mind, yielding has the association of surrendering; it implies loss or defeat. And yet, the 2,000-year-old Taoist text *Tae Te Ching* advises one to "yield and conquer." The apparent paradox of overcoming by yielding is what is addressed in this latest book by grandmaster Leo T. Fong. This text is an essential guide to using yielding or relaxed tension in combative sports as well as actual self-defense situations.

Victory or defeat originates in the mind. Therefore, it is important psychologically to have a clear understanding of yielding. It will facilitate your mastery of the techniques, which Fong teaches in this book.

When force is met by force, the more powerful will prevail. This means that in order to prevail, you would always have to be bigger, stronger or more powerful than your opponent. Yielding is the antithesis of force against force. It can be understood as going with the flow rather than contesting power with power. In yielding, you deflect or redirect an opponent's energy away from yourself and, if necessary, back to your opponent. Because the opponent's force is not being stopped directly, your expenditure of force does not need to exceed or even match that of the opponent. Indeed, a minimal amount of force applied correctly can redirect a substantially greater force. Thus, a Chinese proverb tells us that "four ounces can deflect a thousand pounds." Careful study of the techniques in this book will enable you to apply ounces to move pounds.

SIL LUM MONASTERY

Legend has it that the Si Lum (Cantonese pronunciation) or Shaolin (Mandarin pronunciation) Temple derived its name from the neighboring "young forest" or "*sil lum*." A young forest has flexible branches. The branches bend and regain their shape. An old forest has solid thick branches that do not sway or flex. The flexible branches of a young forest can survive even the strongest winds. The stiff unbending branches of an old tree will be snapped and broken by the force of the wind. The young branches yield and survive; the older ones do not and are broken. Thus, the metaphor or the young branches came to symbolize the techniques of the Sil Lum Temple.

The forest metaphor was quite appropriate and easily understood by the rural inhabitants of ancient China. A more contemporary metaphor might be better suited to today's practitioners of martial arts.

Consider a solid wooden door. It is locked against intruders. If someone wanted to knock it down, he might take a running start and then hurl himself against the door. He may try to open it with his shoulder. Depending on the runner's speed, mass and overall power, he may knock the door open. Or he may bounce—painfully—off the unmoving door. His linear force is met by the proverbially immovable object. Repeated effort will only determine whether his body or the door will give out first. The weaker will break; the stronger will survive.

Now consider a revolving door. Take as much of a running start as you wish. Use as much power and force as you can deliver. But charging the door will send you flying around and down. The door does not attempt to withstand your force. The door revolves, yielding to your force and redirecting you away. This is the essence of yielding. Force is turned harmlessly away. And, yes, as with the turning of the door, a circular motion is used.

Force on force is linear; yielding is circular. The force is not stopped but redirected away in a circle. Pay attention to the large and small circular motions found in the techniques of this book, for they are the keys to yielding.

TIPS FOR USING THIS BOOK

For optimal benefit, there are some guidelines for using this book. If you follow these suggestions, you will maximize your grasp of the concepts and techniques taught within these pages.

Begin by looking at the pictures for a particular technique. Study them and get an overview of what appears to be happening. Notice, in particular, foot placement, hip/waist turning and the circularity of the movements. Next, read the text carefully. Note how the text corresponds to the illustrations.

After studying the text and pictures for a particular technique, sit quietly for a moment or two. Close your eyes and visualize yourself performing the technique. Picture in your mind's eye and visualize yourself performing the technique. Take your time. Do not be in a hurry to rush through this mental practice. It can help to solidify the techniques in your subconscious mind.

The next step is to practice the techniques. Go through the sequence slowly at first. After you feel comfortable with the sequence, gradually increase the speed of your practice. Value proper relaxed movement over frantic rushed activity. If you don't have a partner, visualize one as you perform the movements by yourself. Your mind and imagination are powerful tools, so take full advantage of them.

It has been said that one technique mastered is more useful than one hundred sampled. Take your time as you go through this book. Become completely comfortable with applying one technique before attempting to learn another one.

Diligent, consistent practice will make these concepts and techniques your own. It is for the betterment of all martial arts practitioners that Fong has shared his years of experience. Respect and value his teachings and your skills will definitely move to a higher level.

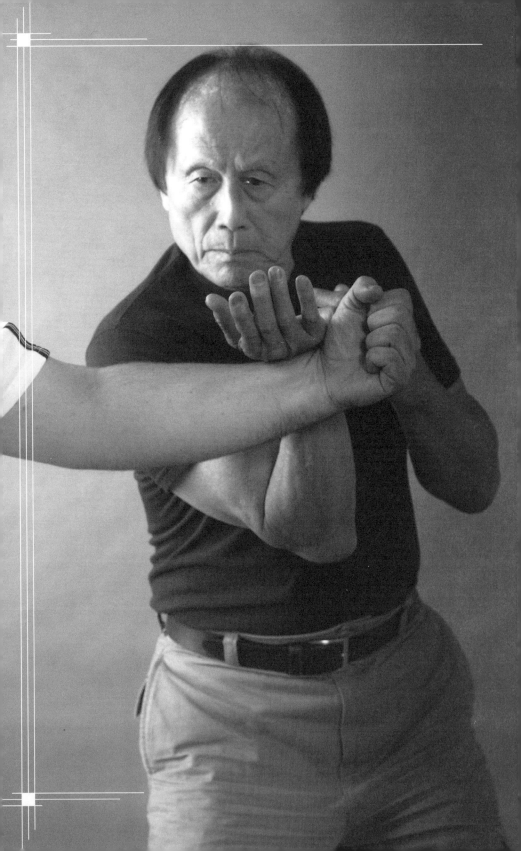

TABLE OF CONTENTS

INTRODUCTION

*B*eyond Kung Fu: Breaking an Opponent's Power Through Relaxed Tension is the synthesis of more than 70 years of experience, research, observation and practice. Relaxed tension is the key to success in all areas of life, from martial arts to daily living. Stress and tension is the root of many illnesses. Stress and tension impede performance in athletics and martial arts. If a martial artist is looking for an edge in competition, relaxed tension is the key to peak performance. If a person is seeking ways to manage stress, relaxed tension is the key relaxation response to many of life's challenges. Whether in the arenas of competition or life, we are constantly tested in how we respond to events as they unfold. The inner skills that require successful answers are best expressed when the body and mind are relaxed and focused. When anger or fear sets in, our responses become tense and anxious. We see this in many boxing matches. When one fighter has the other one in trouble, the one who is about to win by a knockout becomes so excited and anxious to win that he throws a flurry of wild punches. Completely exhausted, his opponent regains his composure and proceeds to knock out the fighter. Relaxed tension enables a fighter to remain relaxed, calm and focused as he methodically measures his opponent.

In the summer of 1985, I was on location shooting a movie in the small town of Lathrop, California. After a long day of filming fight scenes, we wrapped up and headed a few miles north to a Chinese restaurant in Stockton. When we arrived at the restaurant, I realized that I did not have any cash. So I walked up the street to the local Bank of America and took out $100 from the ATM. Just as I completed the transaction, I noticed two young men emerging from around the building. They were about 20 feet away from me, standing several feet apart from each other. As I faced them, I could see bad intentions on their faces, but I reminded myself to remain calm.

Relaxed but focused, I glanced to make sure they were not armed. I noticed that they had on tight sweats and nothing was bulging from their pockets that would indicate they were armed. The next step was to see which one would attack me first. Neither moved. They looked at each other. I looked at both of them. I smiled as I counted the five 20-dollar bills, then walked between them and said, "You boys have a good day." When I was about 10 feet away from them, I looked back and noticed that they had looked at each other, at me and then disappeared down the street in the opposite direction.

That little incident has always remained in my memory. I believe I avoided a mugging by those two young men because I was calm, relaxed and focused. The energy coming from my relaxed demeanor sent out vibrations that caused my potential attackers to doubt whether they should attack their potential victim.

A relaxed demeanor also applies to noncombative situations. In 2004, my urologist informed me that I had prostate cancer. For many people, this would have been a time for panic. But for me, after years of practicing relaxation responses and maintaining relaxed tension in the face of the unexpected, I was calm. I looked at my doctor and calmly asked, "What are the options?" He laid out a plan of action and I chose surgery. My internal response was not one of worry or panic but of precision and strategy. I believe my ability to look at the diagnosis as just another challenge that needs to be overcome with strategy and precision is the reason I rapidly recovered from surgery and overcame some of the debilitating side effects of the cancer. I knew that attitude, as well as precise exercise and nutrition, had a great effect on recovery.

The title of this book, *Beyond Kung Fu*, is appropriate because we often think of kung fu as just a combat art. Yet in the old days, many kung fu masters were also healers. The principle of relaxed tension has more to do with the inner journey than the outer one. I have seen martial arts competitors and Western boxers train exclusively in physical skills, resulting in tremendous stamina and strength. But under pressure, they broke down mentally and emotionally; they lost. The healing aspect of kung fu requires that the healer have all his inner skills in place. Otherwise, he will not be able to draw on his *chi*.

The subtitle of this book, *Breaking an Opponent's Power Through Relaxed Tension*, places emphasis on the paradoxical principle of opposites. When an opponent attacks with force, you do not try to stop him. Instead, you yield to the direction of his force and help him lose balance so you can counterattack. Similar to when a 1000-pound bull charges at a matador, the matador does not stand in front of the bull and try to stop him. Instead, the matador gracefully steps to the side and lets the bull pass by, expending his power. Relaxed tension is the ability to yield and harmonize with an opponent's forward movements so he will be vulnerable to your counterattacks. The principle of yielding and relaxed tension is easier said than done. After 70 years of practice, I am still in the process of evolving, striving and not quite arriving. I still believe that there is much to be learned. There is much to be refined, such as learning more patience and mastering the art of relaxation response. At this juncture, I am convinced that the key to successfully overcoming and transcending an adversary's power is in the ability to yield, blend in and harmonize with your opponent's force. In short, you want to maintain relaxed tension.

This book emphasizes traditional and modern approaches to utilizing relaxed tension in three basic areas: martial arts in street-defense, martial arts in competition, and martial arts in cinema or cinematic fighting. The book will illustrate how relaxed tension is used in the four fighting ranges: kicking, hitting, trapping and grappling. Relaxed tension will be illustrated in defensive, offensive and counteroffensive techniques. The effectiveness of techniques is based on physical strength and emotional content. Any technique that is executed without emotional content is hollow and ineffective. This is where the "chi factor" comes into play because it has an important role in healing and self-defense. There will be a chapter on developing the chi. The book will illustrate the many exercises that will help a person develop the intrinsic energy known as chi. There will also be a chapter on how to implement chi in striking and other combat action and reaction. There is a difference between chi striking and physical punching. The relaxed-tension chi factor enhances the effectiveness of strikes and punches.

Bruce Lee coined the following phrase in his movie classic *Enter the Dragon*. Someone approaches Lee's character and asks, "What is your style?" Lee looks at the man and nonchalantly replies, "Fighting without fighting." Lee illustrates this in the consecutive scene when he suggests that the man go to a nearby island where Lee will show him his style of "fighting without fighting." The man gets in a boat to go to the island and Lee does not. He lets the man drift away, who yells in panic.

Physical confrontation is not the only option. There is a level of martial arts and life skills that take us beyond the traditional definition of kung fu. The key is the ability to remain relaxed, focused, aware and vigilant. Relaxed tension is that component wrapped up in a "nutshell." It is not something that is acquired by telling yourself that you are going to be relaxed. Rather, it is a phenomenon that is developed through repeated practice.

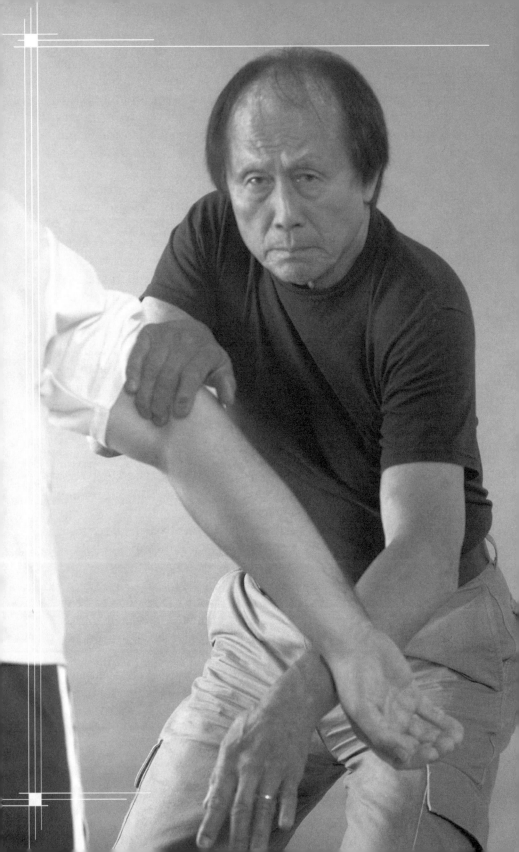

CHAPTER ONE

STAGES OF DEVELOPMENT

After more than 65 years of training in martial arts, one thing that is obvious to me now is the difference between mediocrity and exceptional skill. The martial artist with exceptional skill is the one who has a structured plan of action. The exceptional martial arts skill of Bruce Lee was not by accident or attributed to the gene factor. His great martial arts skill came from dedication to training and a mind that helped him organize and structure a plan of action that would lead him to achieve his goals. There is an old saying, "If you fail to plan, you plan to fail." This is why I can also appreciate the discipline of John Wesley, the founder of the United Methodist Church. It was said that Wesley, like clockwork, arose at 4 a.m. each morning to pray, meditate and read. This structure enabled him to travel thousands of miles on horseback, bringing the message of salvation to frontier America. It's no different in martial arts. When you understand that progress and development is a process, it enhances the growth factor: Your body mechanics and techniques improve; your inner skills, such as mental sharpness and emotional discipline, begin to take shape; and most of all, your mind, body and emotion begin to work as one unit.

I have had the privilege of training with three great martial artists in my lifetime: Bruce Lee, Angel Cabales and Remy Presas. As I reflect on these three great masters, I realize that there are differences between their arts, but there is one common denominator: Each has a structure. Lee articulated the three stages of development to me often. They are developing the tools, refining the tools and dissolving the tools. In later years, as I continued my martial arts journey, I realized there was a fourth stage: expressing the tools. The ultimate stage is the fourth stage. It is reaching a level of proficiency in which all techniques become an expression, much like verbal expression. When you get to the point that you can express your techniques without deliberation but with spontaneity, you are evolving into the fourth stage or the expression stage.

Cabales was a very humble man. He worked in the vineyards and fields of San Joaquin County, California. When I first met him in the late '60s, I was impressed with his martial art: *serrada escrima*. His sticks sang as he whipped them from one angle to the next. After training privately with him for more than a year, I realized that the secret to his proficiency was the way Cabales structured his techniques. His style looked simple, yet it was not. Even though he only had three major components—12 strikes, 12 blocks and 12 counters—Cabales employed a variety of techniques from those three components. As we practiced, I realized that we moved through the three stages of development. I had moved from the stage of developing the tools to the stage of refining the tools to the stage of dissolving the tools. By the end of the year, I was able to free-spar with Cabales. I became aware of my spontaneous response to his attacks, defenses and counters.

I met Presas in 1974 in Manila, Philippines, while filming a movie on location. Presas had many techniques for self-defense, but the foundation of his art was what he called modern *arnis*. His modern arnis was based on 12 strikes. He utilized two sticks about 27 inches long in his practice. From those 12 strikes came many techniques. At the core of modern arnis was one word: flow. Presas could move from stick techniques to empty-hand techniques to kicks without breaking rhythm. In practice one morning, he demonstrated how flow truly works. We were practicing strikes and blocks, moving around the large living room in my apartment. Suddenly, Presas dropped down, applied a scissor-leg sweep and took me down. It was a total surprise because he was able to make that transition without telegraphing his intention. Another incident of flow I remember was when Presas moved from strikes and blocks to trapping and immobilization. In reflecting on all that I had observed later, I realized that his ability to express himself in martial arts terms was based on his core foundation. From that core foundation, Presas moved through the four stages of development in which he was able to express all his basic techniques smoothly and efficiently.

It is important to keep the four stages of development in focus as you move forward. The stages allow you to peel away the nonessentials, discover subtleties, and develop depth and content in the martial arts. One of my favorite pastimes is to watch world-class professional boxers compete. The way they express themselves in a physical way reflects the many years of training in the ability to be spontaneous and the sophisticated way in which they express themselves during offense, defense and counteroffense. As I make this statement, I have in mind one of my favorite boxers, Bernard Hopkins, the former middleweight and light-heavyweight boxing champion. Hopkins has a trademark left jab. In 2001, Hopkins fought Felix Trinidad, another world-class fighting professional. Trinidad could not avoid getting hit by Hopkins' left jab. I remember taping that fight and watching each contestant very closely. What I noticed later was a very subtle movement: Before Hopkins strikes with his left jab, he would slightly dip his body and then jab. The jab hit its mark almost every time. In that small subtle and inconspicuous move, he broke Trinidad's inner rhythm. That little dip was so subtle and inconspicuous that even Trinidad's trainer, his own father, did not know why his son was getting hit. His advice to his son when Trinidad came back to his corner at the end of each round was, "Son, you got to keep your hands up!" Such exceptional skill as Hopkins' comes from moving from one stage to the next. It is what Lee refers to as "from no form to no form."

When you begin the first stage of development, you choose your tools, punches, kicks, stances, etc. As you execute these tools, they feel awkward. However, as you continue to practice and get a hang of what you are doing, you begin to smooth out. Once you have mastered the dynamics of the technique, you begin to move into the refinement stage by continuing to sharpen your tools. Refining the techniques is much like sharpening the ax to cut down a tree. Once the sharpening process is completed, you move into the dissolving stage in which the actual "chopping" begins. It is in the dissolving stage that the application of techniques takes place. The structure suddenly becomes "no structure." Through maturity and constant practice you will eventually be able to express your techniques without deliberation. Every thing becomes the Zen factor. You become the Zen factor when the expression of techniques becomes natural, automatic and spontaneous.

The first stage of development, "developing the tools," is very important. It doesn't matter which system or style you choose because developing the tools is basic and basics are the foundation from which you will build. My martial arts journey began with Western boxing. I fought in individual bouts and tournaments.

When I finally retired from boxing after 25 amateur and intercollegiate bouts in 1952—winning 22 fights, 18 by knockout—I was hired as the athletic director and boxing coach at Ranking Community Center in West Dallas, Texas. Looking back, I realize that I had moved from one stage to the next, even though I did not notice it at the time. My first attempt at boxing was from a book I had bought, *The Fundamentals of Boxing*, by Barney Ross. I read the book from cover to cover. I did as the book had instructed, which was to learn the basic punches and footwork. In my 12-year-old way, I was "developing the tools." I practiced all the punches on a daily basis. My first test came when I was challenged on the school playground and fought one of the school bullies. He came at me swinging hard and wild, but I countered his strikes with straight left jabs. I realized for the first time that attitude can take you only so far; it is the proper tools that get the job done.

I continued to refine my tools. I practiced the left jab, the left hook, the right uppercut and the right cross. I did not feel comfortable using these techniques at first, but as I practiced more and more, the techniques became more natural and spontaneous. I began to supplement the practice of techniques with resistance exercises like push-ups, chin-ups and sit-ups. I later added running for stamina and shadowboxing to develop form and flow. As the years went by, I began to advance in skills and took on tougher opponents. When I had graduated from the third stage, (the dissolving stage of my development), I began to feel the effect of the fourth stage: expression. It was here that free sparring became a weekly routine. It was during free sparring that all the tools and techniques began to come together as a single unit. When an opponent ducked a left hook, I automatically followed up with an uppercut. When an opponent charged in, I would stop-hit with a left jab to set up a right cross.

These automatic responses come only when you practice regularly and look for ways to supplement your training to help refine your techniques. This way, when you move into the dissolving and expression stage, you will be able to perform the techniques with speed, power, timing and relaxed focus. When I came out to California in 1954, I was interested in Eastern martial arts. Growing up, my father had talked about kung fu and other martial arts; I was determined to look into these various arts and see how different and effective they were compared to my boxing skills. When I arrived in Sacramento, California, the only instructions I found was a *jujutsu* class. I had to learn the art from the beginning. We started with falling, rolling and other mat exercises. From there, we moved to defense against various attacks, and by year's end, I was grappling and learning countering and escaping techniques. It was the same when I found a kung fu class and later a *taekwondo* instructor. In each art, I had to move from the developing-the-tool stage to the fourth stage, the expression stage.

Any martial arts practitioner who endeavors to achieve the skills of a champion must be willing to commit himself to developing his skill from stage one through stage four. What I have discovered in my martial arts journey is that you cannot skip any stage and expect to have the complete picture. This is also true in life. From birth to death, life is designed to be lived one stage at a time. When a person is deprived of living a specific stage of his life, he usually encounters personal and psychological problems in later years.

In the following chapters, I will discuss the four stages of development in more detail. I will demonstrate how the four stages of development have an evolutionary effect on you as a committed practitioner of the martial arts. Nothing in life is static. Change is inevitable. Even in traditional martial arts, what was at the beginning and what is now is different. No matter how hard you try to preserve the past, the years bring changes. This is true in martial arts and in all sports. Boxers fight differently today than they did when John L. Sullivan was champion at the turn of the century. Basketball is played differently today than it was 60 years ago. The person who can adapt to changes is a person who grows. When you work within the structure of the stages, your skills will evolve. The qualities that make a proficient martial artist will begin to unfold. And along the way, the skill to win and the skill to succeed will gradually emerge.

CHAPTER TWO

STAGE ONE: DEVELOPING THE TOOLS

Some martial artists begin their martial arts journey with traditional martial arts. As the years go by, they begin to practice a more eclectic approach. This was the case in my situation. I began with traditional kung fu after my collegiate boxing career ended. After years of training in traditional systems, I began to evolve back to boxing. However, there was one difference: I did not rely solely on Western boxing. What emerged as I continued to practice was "street boxing" and later "pressure-point boxing." The evolution to each approach gave me specific skills. In street boxing, I discovered the effectiveness of basic boxing punches in a self-defense situation. In pressure-point boxing, I discovered the effectiveness of hitting knockout points accurately on the body. I also discovered that those boxing skills gave me a formidable delivery system for pressure-point attacks.

In recent years, I discovered the need to develop a nonresistant mind-set and a relaxation response to all situations, whether in a life-threatening situation or in the course of daily activities. The need to yield to an opponent and maintain relaxed tension, relaxed focus, relaxed awareness and relaxed concentration are the core elements that made all the other things work. To be a total person, or a total martial artist, I integrated all I learned in the four stages, starting with developing the tools, to the highest stage of development, expressing the tools. It was in this fourth stage that I realized the value of being completely relaxed while maintaining live tension that can spring into action whenever needed. Being grounded thoroughly in the basics of the art is important. This is why the first stage of development is the key to future success. The basics are the foundation of whatever you do. When things go wrong, you always go back to the basics to regroup. It all begins with a solid foundation.

In this chapter, I will discuss some of the tools needed to develop a foundation for being a proficient martial artist. Developing the skills to be a proficient martial artist is much like building a house; you need a good solid foundation. If the foundation is weak, the house will fall. If it is strong, it will endure intense storms and other natural disasters. It is no different in martial arts. The foundation of a proficient martial artist is a good foundation, and that foundation is built on a good stance. Stances and basic tools will enhance your expressing skills.

TRADITIONAL STANCES

The traditional stances first found their roots in Chinese kung fu and Japanese karate. Both traditions place great emphasis on developing strong stances. Without a strong foundation, the martial artist cannot execute his techniques with power. This was emphasized to me when I was studying *choy lay fut* kung fu in the late '50s under grandmaster Lau Bun. He would have us stand in a horse stance for hours. In fact, he introduced a horse form that we had to do correctly before he would show us hand movements. Although I found that some traditional stances limited my mobility, in the end, they were valuable in developing leg power. This is the reason why moving from one stage of development to the next will reveal what works in specific situations and what doesn't.

FRONT HORSE STANCE

In the front horse stance, your weight is evenly distributed between both legs. The horse stance is valuable in training for leg strength and provides a foundation for supplementary exercises such as standing presses, curls and other lifting exercises. There is a point in combat in which dropping into a horse stance can enhance execution of hand techniques: counterattacks. The sinking of the body provides a solid foundation at the moment the punch or strike makes contact with the target.

SIDE HORSE STANCE

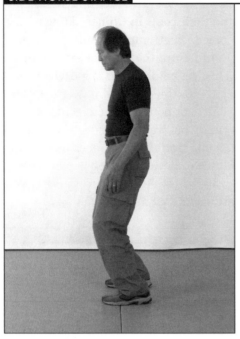

Fighting from a side horse stance can be very effective. The side horse stance provides protection from frontal attacks and at the same time gives you an angle to effectively execute backfists, ridgehand strikes with the thumb side of the hand, side kicks, hook kicks and reverse hook kicks. The legendary Bill Wallace comes to mind as a person who can execute techniques effectively with speed and power from a side horse stance.

CAT STANCE

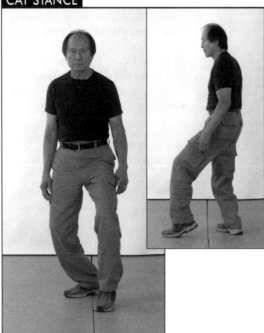

The weight distribution of the cat stance is 90/10. Most of the weight is on the back leg and the front toe is touching the floor. The weight distribution enables a practitioner to utilize his front leg kicks. Also, I have found it effective in lunge punches because it shifts the weight from the left leg to the right so you end up in a front stance. The cat stance can be a launching pad for moving from one position to the next in the course of competition or self-defense.

BACK STANCE

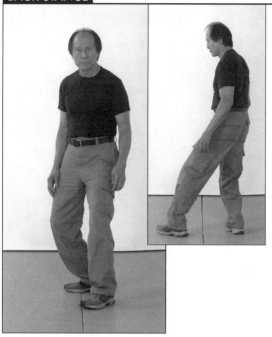

The weight distribution of the back stance is 60/40, with 60 percent of the weight on the back leg. I have found the back stance effective in helping to maintain a relaxed focus in sparring.

FRONT STANCE

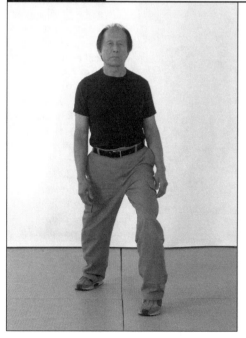

The front stance enhances the reverse punch and front kick in karate. Martial arts such as kickboxing and mixed martial arts utilize a more mobile type of stance with the heel raised and movement from the balls of the feet. Many karate *kata* are performed from the front stance because it gives the kata more physical solidity.

SIDE VIEW OF THE FRONT STANCE

The weight distribution in the front stance is 50/50. Many traditional techniques are executed from the front stance. Some of the great tournament competitors of the '60s and '70s utilized the front stance quite effectively.

THE BOW AND ARROW STANCE

The weight distribution of the bow-and-arrow stance is about 60/40, with most of the weight on the front leg. The front foot is turned inward about 45 degrees, and the back heel is lifted. This stance enables the traditional practitioner to push off the back foot when advancing or shift from one stance to the next. Many utilize this stance because it provides a power base for their techniques.

MODERN STANCES

As I move into the section on modern stances, I need to point out that in the evolutionary process, it is easy to "discard" the old as we embrace the new. In my martial arts journey, the newness and excitement of learning kung fu overshadowed the previous stances I utilized in boxing and other Western martial arts. There are many traditional martial artists who abandoned traditional tools when they discovered the Western martial arts such as boxing and wrestling. Some have even said, "Traditional stances are ineffective. They are too stilted." Although they may not work as well as modern stances in free-sparring situations, nevertheless traditional stance are a great way to develop power in the lower extremities. They are not completely useless.

It was several years later that I realized the value of both traditional and modern stances. Modern stances are more "light-footed" with one leg forward and the other leg placed in the rear. The rear foot with the heel raised is positioned for quick forward motion and lateral moves. Traditional stances are more grounded, meaning the center of gravity is lower and more solid. Modern stances provide mobility, while free-sparring and traditional stances provide a good power base. In practicing traditional stances, I developed the lower body.

Modern stances are designed for speed and mobility, thus the raised back heel, and the focus on "lightness" of feet as demonstrated in the following photos.

ON-GUARD POSITION

The on-guard position is commonly utilized in Western boxing. It is similar in that the hands are held at shoulder height with the elbows resting on the side of the chest. The front leg is slightly bent, while the rear heel is slightly raised. After several years of training in the traditional horse stance, I tend to keep my body slightly lower than most boxing stances. The weight distribution is 50/50. However, advancing forward requires the lead front leg to move forward while the rear heel is used to push off. In intervening years, I have modified the "traditional" modern stance for shifting. For example, if I want to advance, I can step forward with the rear leg to cover distance and add power to punching.

HALF ON-GUARD STANCE

There are several reasons for utilizing the half on-guard stance, which is when the left lead arm is slightly lowered and the right arm is chin high. One of the main reasons for this position is that it enhances my relaxed focus, relaxed tension, and my mental and emotional position. From this position, I maintain some of the traditional power of the horse stance but am able to "roll with the punches." This means that I engage the shoulder as a secondary defense against blows and avoid the so-called *wing chun lop shou* techniques in which the wing chun practitioner grabs and jerks the leading hand of his opponent while striking simultaneously. This stance enables me to strike, defend and counter with minimum telegraphing. It also makes it easier to move in harmony with an opponent's attacks.

THE SOUTHPAW STANCE

The southpaw stance is utilized in boxing for those who are left-handed. The power hand is usually the rear left hand, and the right hand is used for jabs, uppercuts and hooks. Most *jeet kune do* practitioners use this stance because Bruce Lee emphasized it. Lee's logic for using the southpaw stance as its basic stance, especially for right-handers, was his belief that one should put the power hand forward. He believed that the shortest distance between two points was a straight line and the forward hand is closest to your target on an opponent. Although I trained with the great legend from 1962 to 1971 in the Oakland Club, I use the "traditional" on-guard left-lead-hand-forward southpaw stance. When Lee realized that my power hand was in my rear right hand and the left hook was my knockout punch, he allowed me to train that way. You can also utilize the southpaw stance by bringing both hands up chin high.

MODIFIED HORSE STANCE

The modified horse stance allows you to have the best of both worlds because it is a combination of Western and Eastern traditions. You are facing your opponent with only your left side exposed and front heel slightly lifted for a quick forward spring to close the gap between you and your opponent. This stance is used by one of the greatest kickers in the martial arts: Bill Wallace. In addition to the cross-tradition values, the modified horse stance is a great defensive posture. It does not allow your vulnerable areas to be exposed to an attack. Yet from this stance, you can execute all the punches and kicks that are necessary for a competitive edge. It was also a stance used quite effectively by world kickboxing champion Joe Lewis, especially in his point-tournament days. From that stance, he was able to launch his bone-crushing side kicks.

TRADITIONAL HAND POSITIONS

As I reflect back to the early days of my martial arts training, I now realize how much a particular era dictates the way people approach combat situations. The combat methods of World War I were much different than the methods of World War II. It is no different in the martial arts. The era dictates the methodology. Many of the traditional hand positions were born out of a particular era. They were not designed for competition but for the so-called "one-punch kill."

TRADITIONAL KARATE HAND POSITION

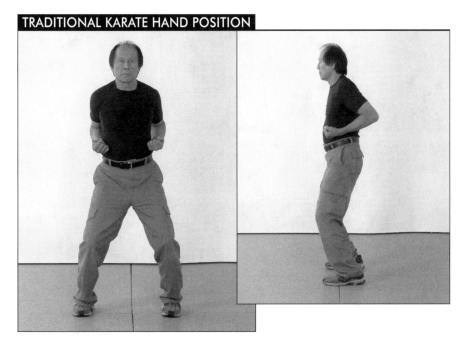

The traditional karate hand position, with both fists above the hips, allows the hip to play a part in generating striking power. This occurs especially when one arm is extended, and the extended arm pulls back toward the hip while the other fist is projected toward the target. The pulling and striking with the snap of the hips is designed to generate tremendous power that can break bones as well as inanimate objects such as boards and bricks. Okinawan karate was developed during the Japanese occupation when all weapons were banned. The natives developed weapons from natural resources. Legend has it that many Okinawan karate masters were able to strike with a reverse punch against the armor of an occupant and kill him inside his armor. Such was the penetrating force of this palm-up and hip-positioned punch.

WING CHUN BI-JON HAND POSITION

The *wing chun bi-jon* position was used by Bruce Lee during his wing chun years. It later evolved into Lee's modified version of wing chun, which he called *Jun Fan gung fu*. The left or right hand can be the lead hand, depending on your preference. The hands are not clenched in a fist but are open. The elbows rest about three inches from the rib cage. This is similar to a karate back stance in which the weight distribution is 60 percent on the back leg and 40 percent on the front leg. This position is designed for proficiency and economy of movement. All movements are kept "tight" around the body. There are no wide-sweeping or wide-swinging techniques. Finger striking is with an open palm, while the striking surface for a closed fist is the last three knuckles in a vertical fist. The snap of the wrist and twisting of the hips generate penetrating power. Lee demonstrated the power of this punch, which some called the "one-inch" punch, when he knocked a person back several feet at the 1967 International Karate Tournament in Long Beach, California. The founder of wing chun theorized that straight punching nullified the round sweeping punches of many kung fu systems. This is the reasoning for this wing chun stance.

TIGER CLAW HAND POSITION

In traditional Chinese kung fu, the tiger-claw hand position is used to claw and rip at an opponent. The techniques were inspired by the original kung fu masters who observed how tigers clawed and ripped at their prey with their claws and teeth. Tiger claw kung fu is an effective self-defense approach once mastered. The grasping and ripping motion can inflict damage to an attacker's eyes, throat and groin. The claw can be used to immobilize the wrists and arms so the defender can't execute many other counter-techniques. Tiger claw masters have been known to lift heavy jars filled with sand and metals balls with just their fingers. Others have trained to strengthen their fingers by stabbing their empty hands into a bucket of steel ball bearings. Many of the kung fu systems in Chinese were designed for self-defense rather than sports competition.

MODERN HAND POSITIONS

When I refer to modern hand positions, I am referring to holding the hands up near the chin, as opposed to traditional hand positions, which keep the hands at the waist. The waist-hand position is prevalent in all *kata* in kung fu and karate. In modern hand positions, the hand is held high and relaxed as in the boxing, kickboxing, *muay Thai* or *jeet kune do* postures and enable the defender to utilize slips, side steps and ducks as well as blocks. The hard styles of karate and kung fu place strong emphasis on blocks. Often the hard-blocking motion can damage the attacker's arm or leg because the block is often used as an attack weapon.

THE SHUFFLE

The hand position and the shuffle are executed as one unit. In the modern hand positions in which the rear hand acts as a guard and the front hand is utilized as the lead weapon, the shuffle and the hand movements work as one single unit. The footwork helps close the gap while the front hand is attacking the target.

RELAXED POSTURE

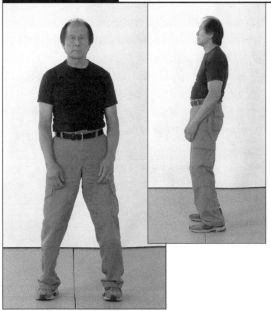

One of the key principles in self-defense is maintaining a relaxed focus and a relaxed awareness. The relaxed posture is one of the most effective ways to maintain relaxed tension, yet not be tense and tight. This posture communicates to a potential adversary that you are not looking for trouble. It can deceive him into a state of complacency if he is determined to attack. From this posture, you can respond to all attacks, provided you stay alert and alive.

CONTEMPLATIVE POSTURE

The contemplative posture does not leave you as exposed as the relaxed posture. From this posture, you can deflect and block kicks and punches as efficiently as if you were in an orthodox on-guard stance.

Yet, by your stance, you are communicating non-threatening and passive vibrations. Stances very often define attitudes. A "chip on the shoulder" attitude can attract unwelcome trouble. You as a defender have much at stake. It is better to discourage a physical confrontation than encourage one. Postures and stances are often the key to allaying fear or anger.

TRADITIONAL DEFENSIVE POSITIONS

In the following defensive position, the defender is executing an upper block from a horse stance. The block can also be executed from a front stance or back stance. Traditional blocks are designed to be executed with power. The mind-sets of the old masters are that blocks can also be used as counteroffensive weapons. The traditional blocks demonstrated in this section can be executed from any stance, but it all depends on the situation and the direction in which your opponent is attacking.

HORSE STANCE UPPER BLOCK

The upper block from a horse stance is a strong response to an overhead attack. This block is commonly practiced in traditional martial arts in one-step sparring, *kata* and in free fighting. The upper block is designed to attack while in a defensive mode. There are practitioners of traditional karate who can break an arm with an upper block, especially if the attacker performs a powerful overhead attack. This block can also be executed from a front stance, back stance and cat stance.

HORSE STANCE OUTWARD BLOCK

The outward block can be used to stop wide punches and roundhouse kicks. The edge of the wrist can add additional pain to the attack if the block hits a sensitive nerve in the opponent's leg. The outward block can be utilized as an offensive weapon. Like all traditional karate blocks, they are executed with power. The intention is to smash and break.

HORSE STANCE DOWNWARD BLOCK

The traditional karate downward block is used to block front kicks, side kicks and other low-level attacks. It can also be used as a counteroffensive weapon against a wrist-grab attack by pulling the opponent abruptly toward you and chopping down on his forearm or other pressure points.

HORSE STANCE INWARD BLOCK

The inward block is executed by an inward snapping motion to block all incoming straight attacks, especially reverse punches to the body and head. It works best against linear attacks. The edge of the closed fist makes contact with the attack limb. The inward block is a very effective offense and counteroffensive weapon.

CIRCULAR PALM-UP BLOCK

The circular palm-up block is executed by blocking in a clockwise direction against an imaginary strike. If utilizing the right arm, you go in a counterclockwise direction (1-2). In the follow-through, the circular block can also be used to trap a kicking attack once you stop the momentum of the kick. You do this with a scooping motion and then by lifting up his leg to cause the kicker to lose balance. You can also do a circular palm-up block in a horse stance.

CIRCULAR SCOOP BLOCK

The circular scoop block does exactly what it says. When defending against a front or side kick, you execute a scooping motion to trap the leg and cause the attacker to lose balance (1-3).

MODERN DEFENSIVE POSITIONS

The modern defensive positions are different than the traditional karate blocks in that the modern defensive positions utilize body movements to make the attacker miss while being in a position to counterattack. The purpose is to off-balance the attacker as he overshoots his intended target. The entire concept is based on an old Chinese adage: "When someone attacks you, use four ounce of deflection against four thousand pounds of force." In other words, yield to your opponent's attack rather than meet force with force. Evading and eluding is quite effective against powerful attacks. Morihei Ueshiba, the father of *aikido*, expressed this concept quite eloquently when he said, "If your opponent strikes with fire, counter with water, becoming completely fluid and free-flowing. Water, by its nature, never collides with or breaks against anything. On the contrary, it swallows up any attack harmlessly."

The shoulder roll is one of several effective defensive maneuvers in a Western boxer's defensive arsenal. The key to implementing this technique effectively is to be completely relaxed and aware. Timing is of the essence. Relaxation is key to timing.

Timing comes from many sources; one of them is through practice. The more relaxed and aware you are, the more sensitive you are to when your opponent will attack. The great boxer Sugar Ray Robinson once said, "When I start seeing openings, I know it's time to retire." What Robinson was saying is that defense is based partly on sight and partly on instinct. Instinct is the ability to feel and sense your opponent's intention. Like the adage suggests, you want to "see with your skin." Such sensitivity comes from the ability to be relaxed and aware. When you lose that sense of quiet awareness, you lose sight of your opponent. The shoulder roll is conducive to this relaxation response to attacks. The mere rolling of the shoulder at the point of attack will make your opponent miss and put him in a vulnerable striking distance for your counterattacks. Posture is important when you want to roll inside of your opponent's attack. The following photos demonstrate the type of posture or on-guard position needed to implement the shoulder roll effectively. When your opponent attacks, you want to shift the target and make him miss so he can put himself into your line of counterattack.

THE SHOULDER ROLL

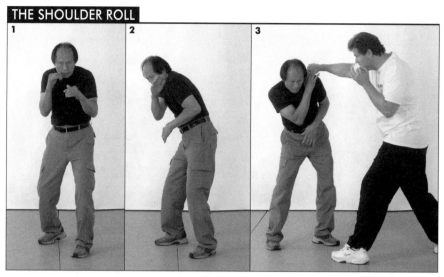

The right hand is held at shoulder height. The left hand is held to the side. From this position, you can "stick" with a left jab and shift. The entire body should be relaxed but ready for any attack (1). Assuming your opponent has just completed a right punch attack, roll your shoulder away and in the forward direction of the punch. Simultaneously deflect the punch with the right hand, which will put you in a position to counter with uppercuts and hooks (2). The attacker executes a right punch; the defender rolls and makes the attack miss his mark. From this position the defender can counter with a left uppercut, a right uppercut, a right backfist or a number of low kicks and sweeps (3).

INSIDE PARRY AGAINST A RIGHT PUNCH

The inside parry is executed by brushing an attacker's right punch outward as the defender shifts slightly to his right. It is important to yield and maintain relaxed tension when you brush the attacking arm aside. All movements should be fluid, light and yielding, like water.

The purpose of the inside deflection is to direct the attacker's arm away from the intended target. Unlike the hard block that is designed to knock the attacker's punch away, the deflection is much more subtle and soft. The defender feels the direction of the attacker's power and goes with the flow. The defender moves his body slightly away from the path of the punch as he deflects it. As soon as the punch has expended its power, the defender is in the position to counter with either hand. Again, sensitivity plays an important role in deflecting punches. Once the attacker begins to withdraw his attacking arm, the defender will initiate his counterattack.

DEFLECTION IN THE ON-GUARD POSITION

The on-guard position is designed for blending with the opponent's attack. The right hand is shoulder height and the left hand is positioned to the side of the chest. The entire body is relaxed but ready and aware.

INSIDE DEFLECTION AGAINST A RIGHT PUNCH

In this photo, the defender demonstrates the position of the deflecting hand against an imaginary right punch.

INSIDE DEFLECTION AGAINST AN ACTUAL RIGHT PUNCH

The attacker on the right executes a right punch; the defender on the left deflects the punch. As the back of the defender's palm makes contact with the attacker's punch, the defender moves his body slightly to his left to go with the attacker's power.

The movements in the above photo sequences are very subtle. When the defender comes in contact with the attacker's arm, he must remain relaxed and, with minimum force, turn his body slightly as the hand touches his attacking arm, as if he is guiding his attacker past the intended target. The entire process is not about power; it is all about a relaxation response to whatever attack an adversary wishes to launch. By blending into an opponent's energy and power direction, you are a step ahead and in control.

In Chapter Three, I will discuss some of the factors that put emotional substance into the techniques. Proficiency in martial arts demands depth and refinement. Without inner substance, techniques are just mere movements. It is less important how you hold your hands or where you place your feet. It is more important in how you express those techniques. It is very important to have emotional, mental and spiritual substance in all you do.

CHAPTER THREE

STAGE TWO: REFINING THE TOOLS

In this chapter, I will discuss some of the inner content needed to take the tools to the next level. When you reach the refinement stage, it is not about looking for new techniques or adding on to them but rather taking what is useful and refining them. Abraham Lincoln was once asked what he would do if he had five hours to chop down a tree. He replied, "I would spend four hours sharpening the ax." Once you have defined the tools and begun to develop them, the refinement stage begins.

THE CHI FACTOR

When people consider human function and the human body, they often think in terms of two major components: the physical and the mental. However, in my own martial arts journey, I have realized that totality of development cannot be complete until you acknowledge other components that are present. Instead of being just composed of the mind and body, you are also made up of spiritual and emotional energy. This perspective is not just an "Eastern thing." The Chinese refer to the energy presence as *chi*, the Japanese call it *ki* and Indians identify this presence as *prana*. If you think about it, chi is present in all life. Energy runs the entire universe. It is no different in your body. Your health and daily functions are determined by the flow of energy or chi. In China, when an ill person visits the doctor, the first thing the doctor will check is the "blockage of the chi." The doctor will start with the energy meridians and pressure points. Every organ in the body is connected to a pressure point. Often, the patient walks away feeling much better once the blockage is unblocked. The Chinese medical community also acknowledges that stress or tension is the root of all diseases. They refer to this condition as "dis-ease." Stress and tension impedes the flow of chi. When the chi is unblocked and allowed to flow again, the symptoms disappear. There is a relationship between chi flow and martial arts proficiency.

I have discovered there are two ways to project power in martial arts: one is through pure physical power and the other is through chi power. Chi power is more subtle and effortless but also more lethal, whereas pure physical power can render an opponent unconscious and often cause serious physical injuries. However, in chi striking, the damage is more internal, whereas in physical punching, the injuries are more external.

A case in point: In one of my annual seminars, I demonstrated the difference between physical punching and chi striking. In physical punching, I was able to physically move the person I was punching, whereas in chi striking, the recipient did not move. When asked which was more painful, he said "the chi strike."

The difference in chi striking and physical punching is that striking requires the striker to be completely relaxed. The mind and emotion play an integral part in the process. The striker must project the chi to the intended target. The arms and legs are mere vehicles to project the chi power to the target, while muscle power is important in physical punching. There are some who boast that they can lift 300 pounds while bench-pressing. They have the physiques of a bodybuilder. In contrast, many chi-based martial arts practitioners are either skinny and puny looking or overweight.

Lee was once asked in an interview, "What is the difference between karate and kung fu?" He broke into that famous Lee smile and replied, "Karate is like getting hit with a steel bar. Kung fu is like getting hit with a steel ball on the end of a chain." Thus, the reference to "hard style" karate and "soft style" kung fu. One has a smashing effect, while the other has a whipping effect.

TENSION VERSUS RELAXED FOCUS

Tension in offense and defense is counterproductive. When a defender is too tight, he will telegraph any counterattacks. If the offense is too tight and rigid, the attacker will again telegraph his intention, and if a blow should land, it will do so with less power. Tension in defense and offense rob techniques of explosiveness. Proficiency in combat is based on the four F's:

Form
Flow
Footwork
Feeling

Tension will impede the Four F's of combat proficiency. The fighter must be relaxed at all times, in defense, offense and counteroffense. The ability to remain relaxed and focused is the key to explosive and penetrating power.

TENSE ON-GUARD POSITION

The defender is in a tight, tense on-guard posture (1). The defender uses his arms as a shield, keeping them tight and tense to ward off the blows (2). A tight, tense shield defense does not always offer protection. The attacker can still jerk the arm down and strike to a pressure point or perform a strike like a backfist (3).

CONTRASTING FROM TENSE TO RELAXED TENSION

In the following sequence of photos, the defender demonstrates the fluidity of a relaxed-tension approach to various attacks. When the body and mind are relaxed and in motion, the body will go with the flow of the attacker's movements. In harmonizing with the opponent's attack, the defender neutralizes the attack.

UTILIZING THE WEAVE

Bobbing and weaving can create an inner rhythm that will allow the defender to keep pace with the opponent's attack. Former world heavyweight boxing champion Joe Frazier—who had three epic bouts with Muhammad Ali in the 1970s—was known for his bobbing-and-weaving approach. He had an inner rhythm that made his famous left hook a lethal weapon. Like Jack Dempsey before him, Frazier's movements were almost musical in beat as he defended, countered and attacked with fluidity (1-3).

DEFLECTING

When the body and mind are relaxed and focused, the defender can move from bobbing and weaving to deflecting and countering as demonstrated in the five deflecting photos. When the body and mind are relaxed, a martial artist can move with flow and make one transition to the next without breaking his inner rhythm. The defender can choose to counterattack at any time (1-5). In the fifth photo of the deflecting series, the defender chooses to punch the ribs. Relaxed focus and relaxed tension allow the defender to use each movement as a launching pad for the next, regardless of whether it's offensive or aggressive defense. The defender does not have to break rhythm and regroup; every movement is an automatic expression, much like a sound or an echo.

HARDNESS VERSUS YIELDING

Sensitivity is an integral part of upper-level martial arts proficiency. Defense and counteroffense are more than just visual; they are also feeling and sensitivity. It is the ability to "see with your skin." In other words, once your opponent comes in contact with any part of you, you will know exactly where to go from that point. When I was training with Lee, one of the drills we often did was called *chi sao*, which translates to "sticky hands." Chi sao is an integral part of the *wing chun* kung fu system. With chi sao, you try to develop sensitivity to an opponent's attacks and adhere to his limbs like "flypaper." In this drill, Lee would always say, "When you feel emptiness, strike!" It took me years of training to realize the depth of that statement.

Sensitivity skills are not based totally on touching your opponent's body. It is also a feeling that I refer to as a spiritual connection to your opponent. Fighting is a form of communication; there is a connection during the encounter even though the other person's intention is to inflict harm on you.

HARDNESS AGAINST AN OVERHEAD STRIKE

The attacker executes an overhead strike. The defender responds with a hard upper block (1). The attacker is able to exploit the defender's tenseness and redirect and counter with an uppercut (2).

SOFT-YIELDING RESPONSE TO AN OVERHEAD ATTACK

The defender is in an on-guard position while the attacker is ready to execute an overhead attack (1). As the attacker executes an overhead attack, the defender remains relaxed and calm until the attacker commits. The defender moves in harmony with the attacker and deflects the punch (2). The defender counters with a right hook to the attacker's temple (3).

HARD RESPONSE TO A STRAIGHT PUNCH

The attacker is in an on-guard position in preparation for a straight punch (1). The attacker executes a straight punch. The defender blocks hard with an outward block (2). The attacker takes advantage of the defender's overcommitment of his energy and redirects his attack into an uppercut (3).

SOFT-YIELDING RESPONSE TO A STRAIGHT PUNCH

The defender is in a relaxed-focus on-guard position (1). The attacker throws a straight right punch. The defender moves to the attacker's right, yielding to the direction of the punch. The defender lightly places his right hand on the attacking arm (2). The defender guides the attacker's arm down and up as he steps to his left, ready for a counterstrike. This movement must be very soft, as light as a fly that lands on your arm, but with lightness and softness, you guide the attack arm and adhere to it like glue as you complete the counter (3-4). The defender gently pulls the attacker's arm and executes a shovel punch to the attacker's ribs (5). The defender completes the ribs punch, and from this point with flow, he simultaneously strikes the arm with his left palm and executes a backfist strike to the temple (6). The combination of the arm strike and temple strike shuts off the flow *chi*, much like turning off a switch on your light panel.

HARD RESPONSE TO A FRONT KICK

1

2

3

4

The defender is in an on-guard position, slightly tense (1). The attacker executes a front kick while the defender blocks hard and overcommits his energy and power (2). As the defender blocks hard, the attacker yields to his block by moving the attacking leg to his right and preparing for a left punch counter (3). The attacker completes his attack with a left punch to the defender's chin (4).

SOFT-YIELDING RESPONSE TO A FRONT KICK

1

2

3

4

The defender is in a relaxed-focus on-guard position (1). The attacker throws a front kick while the defender slides subtly to his right and deflects the kicking leg to his left (2). As the attacker's foot hits the floor, the attacker performs a left punch. The defender rolls to his own left slightly and prepares his left hand to immobilize the attacker's right arm (3). The defender gently traps and pulls the attacker's left arm and simultaneously counterstrikes with a right punch to the ribs (4).

When a martial artist utilizes the yielding and relaxation response to attacks, he has a decided advantage over an opponent who bases his entire attack on power and raw strength. In the game of scissor, rock, paper, if you were to add water to the game, water will win every time. Water yields and blends, so must the martial artist. It takes years of training to untrain a tense reaction to threatening situations, whether it be real or imagined.

Footwork is also an important aspect of implementing the principles of yielding and blending. The footwork must be subtle and in sync with the rest of the body's movements. The key to developing yielding and relaxed tension in all things is the chi principle of movement. The chi principle of movement is: "Movement in stillness, stillness in movement." In a threatening situation, you move, but internally you are in the stillness mode. Whereas in meditation, you are externally in stillness, but the inner person is in movement. Again, the *yin* and *yang* principle is in operation.

The left hook or right hook punch is one of the most powerful punches in the boxing arsenal. What makes this punch so lethal is that the receiver loses sight of the punch as it angles to its intended target. The hook is also executed by lifting your heel and turning your body as the punch is delivered. It is a punch that naturally utilizes the polarity principle of chi striking. The lifting of the heel as you execute the hook adds to the chi flow, thus making the punch much more powerful. Again, the best way to neutralize the effect of the hook punch is to yield by moving in the same direction of the power.

HARD-YIELDING RESPONSE TO A HOOK-PUNCH ATTACK

The defender is in an on-guard position, slightly tense in anticipation of an attack (1). The attacker launches a right hook, but the defender blocks hard to stop the punch (2). The attacker takes advantage of the overly powerful inward block and traps the blocking arm, counterattacking with a reverse hammerfist to the defender's jaw (3).

SOFT-YIELDING RESPONSE TO A HOOK-PUNCH ATTACK

The defender is in an on-guard position. He is completely relaxed but focused (1). The opponent attacks with a right hook punch. The defender leans slightly to his left and lightly guides and deflects the punch with his left hand. The defender also subtly brings his right hand underneath the left and traps the attacker's wrist (2). The defender quickly jerks the attacker's arm in preparation for the next move (3-4). The defender attacks his opponent's arm to set up for the finishing blow (5). From the previous technique, the defender quickly completes the counteroffense with a backfist strike to the attacker's temple (6).

Responding to a hook-punch attack with a hard block puts you in an overcommitted position. When you overcommit to an attack, if the attacker is skilled in trapping, you will be vulnerable to a potential knockout. By yielding to your opponent's power, you blend into his sphere and are able to control his every move. Again, it is much more sophisticated to feel rather than see, or as some say, "Seeing with your skin."

In order to continue to grow and elevate your fighting skills, techniques must be refined over and over. Every facet of your being must constantly undergo the process of refinement. I first took interest in Western boxing at age 12 when I bought the book *The Fundamental of Boxing* by Barney Ross. I was fascinated by the various punches presented in the book: the left jab, the left hook, the right uppercut and the right cross. Ross was right-handed, so his left hand was his lead hand while his left foot was forward. From this posture, he executed the four basic boxing punches. For months, I practiced the four punches, especially the left jab and the left hook. As I continued to practice on a daily basis by hitting a pillowcase stuffed with old clothes, I noticed that the jabs and hooks became more natural. When I got into fights on school playgrounds, I met my opponents' wild swings and rushes with jabs and hooks. I had an advantage over the untrained bullies. But in my first formal boxing match, an opponent much taller and heavier than me beat me.

Disappointed, I began to reflect on why I was beaten. What came to me was further refinement in my punching skills but also footwork, mental attitude and emotional control. In that first match, I took the fight to my bigger opponent, which was a mistake. I began to realize the need to keep distance and place emphasis on developing timing. I realized that I had just scratched the surface and that there was much more to developing fighting skills than hitting a stuffed pillow. When I speak of refinement, I am referring to the process of sharpening the punches, kicks, blocks and all the attributes that enhance proficiency. Every movement is connected to the mental, emotional, physical and chi process. I still remember the scene in Lee's movie *Enter The Dragon* when he was teaching a young boy how to kick. The boy kept kicking repeatedly but not really getting it, so Lee said to him, "More emotional content." A punch is more than just a punch, a kick is more than just a kick; a punch and a kick is the sum total of a person's emotion, mind, body and focus. As simple as a left jab looks, it takes many years to perfect it to the point in which the practitioner can deliver it with total commitment and without deliberation and doubt. Refinement is the process in which each technique is sharpened until the mind, body, emotion, chi and timing becomes one unit at the point of expression. Refinement is a lifetime process. The key is practice, practice, practice and more practice.

CHAPTER FOUR

STAGE THREE: DISSOLVING THE TOOLS

In this chapter, I will discuss the "art of structure without structure." This statement may sound like "double talk," but if you reflect on the logic, it does make a lot of sense. Every journey begins with the first step. In the martial arts journey, you begin with the choice of tools or techniques. In order to enhance the development of the techniques or tools, structuring is one of the best ways to start. Structuring is much like having a teacher who has a lesson plan, but as the class progresses through the day, he or she may very well go beyond the structure of that lesson plan. Or in the game of football, every team has a playbook. The playbook helps the players know their positions. But once the action starts, they may have to deviate from the original plan because an opposing player may be where the other team had not anticipated. Adjustment to the original play must be made, but in the adjustment, the player does not use a new play but merely makes a small adjustment.

In martial arts, you must have structure so you can cover all the basics. Structure allows you to focus more on specifics rather than just "shotgun" your training—you know everything but you are not particularly skilled in it. When your techniques are refined, you can begin to dissolve the structure in the middle of challenging situations. Another example of "structure without structure" are kata in traditional martial arts. Kata are valuable in developing the foundation in the first stage of development. Every move is prearranged with specific attacks; however, a kata would be ineffective if used as a spontaneous attack. The defender must be able to glean from the kata specific techniques that can defend and counter the attack. Dissolving the tools may challenge you to pull techniques from the kata that would be out of context from the original intention of the form and refine it within the scope of free expression. In other words, kata are merely a guide or a structure from which you work, but they do not require you to be confined within that structure.

Free fighting is the stage in which the practitioner can express his or her techniques without deliberation. Dissolving the tools is the first step in achieving that level of skill. One of the first steps you must take to dissolve the tools is attitude. The speed of your progression is not determined by your aptitude but by your attitude. In order to reach that level of skill in which you can counter quickly, you must be relaxed and ready. Attitude sets the stage for dissolving and expressing.

POSTURE NO. 1: NATURAL STANCE

A person's attitude will determine the kind of posture or stance he will choose in a confrontational situation. Posture and stance communicate attitude, and attitude determines the posture.

In the natural stance, you stand completely relaxed with your hands to the side. However, even in this relaxed natural stance, you must be mentally alert and vigilant. Have a mental picture and emotional connectedness to your environment. If there is an opponent in front of you with an adversarial intention, you want to be ready to change positions in case he tries to "cheap-shot" you. Once you have reached the dissolving stage of development, you should be able to have the reflexive action to deflect, dissolve and counter any potential attack. One of the advantages of continuous refinement of techniques or tools is the adaptation factor. In other words, no matter what stance or posture you choose, you can launch a counteroffense from that position.

NATURAL STANCE AGAINST A PUNCHING ATTACK

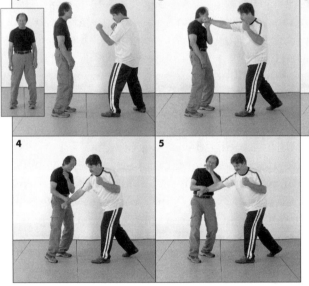

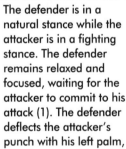

The defender is in a natural stance while the attacker is in a fighting stance. The defender remains relaxed and focused, waiting for the attacker to commit to his attack (1). The defender deflects the attacker's punch with his left palm, and at the same time, he slides his feet to his left and away from the path of the blow. The defender maintains a calm and relaxed mind-set (2). As the defender deflects the attacker's blow with his left palm, he slips his right hand underneath his left hand and immobilizes the attacker's wrist. He pulls the attacker forward to set him up for the completion of the cycle (3). As the defender pulls the attacker forward, the defender will position himself for the next strike (4). As the defender pulls the attacker's arm, the defender will strike with his left elbow against the defender's elbow to disable it (5).

NATURAL STANCE AGAINST A KICKING ATTACK

The attacker assumes a fighting pose. The defender remains in a natural and relaxed ready stance (1). The attacker executes a front kick, and the defender responds by stepping slightly to his left and deflecting the power of the kick (2). The defender follows through with a left jab (3). The attacker blocks the left jab, and the defender uses the attacker's blocking momentum to circle underneath the attacker's wrist with his left hand (4). The defender jerks the attacker's arm down and pulls it to set up for the finishing blow (5). The defender completes the sequence with a right uppercut punch to the attacker's chin (6).

NATURAL STANCE AGAINST AN OVERHEAD ATTACK

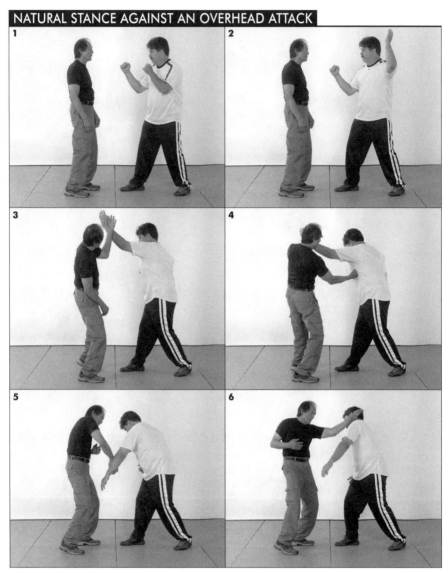

The attacker assumes a fighting pose. The defender is in a natural, relaxed-alert, nonthreatening posture (1). The attacker raises his left arm to attack. The defender will not anticipate the strike or tense up; he remains mentally neutral until the attacker commits to an attack (2). The defender intercepts the attacker's strike by moving to his right and deflecting the punch. At the same time, he adheres to the attacker's wrist with the left palm to set up for the next movement (3). The defender follows through with a uppercut to the attacker's ribs (4). The defender circles the attacker's arm and strikes the attacker's arm with his right hand (5). From the previous photo, the defender completes the sequence with a right backfist to the jaw (6).

POSTURE NO. 2: CONTEMPLATIVE STANCE

One important point to emphasize: Defending against an attacker, whether that attack is intense or aggressive, the defender must remain relaxed and focused. The second point to emphasize is that one punch or one kick may not be enough to stop a determined attacker. In many of the sequences, I'll include several follow-through blows. However, the combination of punches must flow from one point to the next. Jerky motions and regrouping after each blow will be less effective against a skilled attacker. In the art of yielding, the focus is on creating a series that flows from one blow to the next fluidly and smoothly with minimum telegraphing. This is what I call the "chi approach." One of the prerequisites of the chi approach is being relaxed while executing the techniques. This is where the refinement stage is so important. In the chi approach, your focus is on "effortless efficiency."

CONTEMPLATIVE POSTURE AGAINST A RIGHT PUNCH

The attacker assumes a fighting stance. The defender assumes a contemplative posture with his left arm across his lower chest and his right elbow resting on his left hand with the right hand under his chin. Again, the defender must remain relaxed, calm and cool to communicate a nonthreatening attitude (1). The attacker strikes with a right punch, but the defender deflects the blow slightly outward and upward (2). The defender smoothly transitions into a palm strike on the attacker's jaw. He must remain relaxed (3). The defender follows with a right punch to the body to get the opponent to bend forward to set up a knee strike (4). The defender follows with a knee strike to the face to complete the sequence (5).

CONTEMPLATIVE POSTURE AGAINST A RIGHT PUNCH

The attacker assumes a fighting stance. The defender assumes a contemplative nonthreatening posture (1). The attacker initiates the attack with a right punch. The defender deflects the blow (2).The defender does not strike immediately. Instead, he pauses briefly for the attacker to retract the attacking arm before following through with a hammerfist to the jaw (3). The defender follows through with a second punch—an uppercut to the chin (4). The defender continues the flow with a right-hand neck-immobilization strike and a right-knee strike to the body (5).

CONTEMPLATIVE POSTURE AGAINST A KICK

The attacker assumes a fighting stance. The defender remains relaxed and calm in a contemplative posture (1). The attacker initiates a kick, and the defender pivots to the left and scoop blocks the kick (2). The defender follows through with a throat-strike counter (3).

POSTURE NO. 3: CROSS-ARM STANCE

The cross-arm stance is another nonthreatening posture. Although it may have defensive implications to an adversary, it is intended to look passive but the defender is actually alert and aware. It is a great position to launch a defensive attack or a counter. Again, the key to success in all the nonthreatening postures is the ability to remain relaxed and aware. Attitude often communicates a variety of vibes. A negative attitude can send out hostile vibes, while a serene and relaxed attitude can send out nonthreatening vibes, which in turn can defuse a potential fight.

CROSS-ARM POSTURE AGAINST A RIGHT PUNCH

The attacker is in an on-guard stance. The defender remains in a nonthreatening cross-arm pose (1). The attacker launches a right punch, which the defender blocks. When blocking, the defender does not use hard force; he lets his body just dissolve the attack so the attacker's arm remains attached to his arm, setting up the defender's counterstrike (2). Using his sense of feeling, the defender counterattacks when he senses that the attacker is about to retract the attacking arm. Timing and accuracy is important in counterattacks. In this photo, the defender pause just long enough to sense the attacker's initial move to withdraw before exploding with a body punch (3). Bruce Lee reminded me more than once in practice: "When you feel emptiness, attack!" The defender continues the flow and executes an uppercut to the chin (4). In self-defense, the best way to terminate a long fight is to punch in combinations to key pressure points. Punching in angles can enhance the chance of a decisive victory. The defender continues the combination with a left hook to the jaw (5). The combination in this sequence is designed for a quick knockout. The body punch is one of the "switches" that will shut off an opponent's "electrical system." The uppercut and the left hook will be the final blows to shut down *chi* flow.

Defending against a kick is no different than defending against a punch. Most kickers lead you to believe that they have a competitive advantage when they specialize in kicking. Most defenders who are not familiar with kicks will be intimidated by kicks. Once you develop both the lower-body and upper-body awareness to attacks, kicks and punches are the same as far as your inner-defensive awareness is concerned. The ability to move from one range to the next is the key to avoid getting kicked.

CROSS-ARM POSTURE AGAINST A KICK

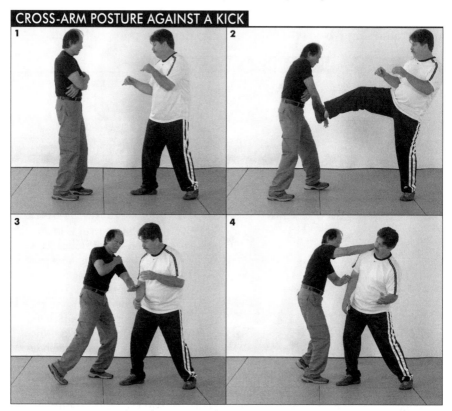

The attacker is in an on-guard position in preparation for an attack. The defender remains calm and relaxed in a cross-arm posture (1). The attacker executes a kick, and the defender deflects the kick by sliding slightly to the right (2). Please note that there is a difference between blocking and deflecting. In blocking, you use force as if to attack the attacking limb, whereas in deflecting, you dissolve the attacker's force by moving in the direction of his attack. The deflection will act as a subtle redirection away from the intended target. The defender traps the attackers arm to nullify a follow-through punch (3). The defender ends the encounter with a hammerfist strike to the opponent's jaw or his gall bladder meridian (4).

Remember, emotional content plays an important role in all aspects of defense, offense and counteroffense. Controlling your emotions will determine the accuracy of your punches and the success of your defense. Nothing impedes the ability to remain calm than an out-of-control emotional response. Anger, fear and a hostile attitude can cause anxiousness. It is best to remain emotionally neutral.

POSTURE NO. 4:
RELAXED ON-GUARD POSTURE (ONE HAND TO THE CHIN)

The relaxed on-guard posture, with one hand to the chin, can communicate mixed feelings. However, this stance allows the defender to be ready for defense, offense or counters. This stance does not totally communicate a combative stance. It might convey a message to the attacker that the defender is not totally ready. This is one of my favorite stances because it enables me to be relaxed but combat ready. Skillful combat is a game of chess. Strategy always prevails over pure strength and killer instinct.

ON-GUARD RELAXED POSTURE

The attacker is ready to execute an overhead attack. The defender is totally relaxed but vigilant and ready in the on-guard stance (1). As the blow descends, the defender slides to his left and helps the attacker continue his downward attack (2). The defender intercepts the attacker's attacking arm with his right hand in preparation for a counterkick (3). The defender jerks the attacker's arm and simultaneously kicks the attacker's knee to immobilize it (4).

In the following sequence of photos, the defender demonstrates the effectiveness of remaining relaxed and alert. The key to staying a step ahead of your opponent's attack is to be totally relaxed and alert so you can blend into his every move and turn each move into a defense or counterattack. In other words, whatever he "throws" at you, you can turn into an advantage. It is what I call "martial arts imitating life." In life, I adhere to the philosophy that once you acquire sufficient inner skills, you can turn "lemons into lemonade," "obstacles in opportunities" or "problems into projects." This is true in the art of yielding or the art of nonresistance. When you develop sensitivity and remain relaxed and focused, you can use your opponent's energy against him. In other words, whatever the opponent tries to do to you, you use it as a springboard for a counterattack. In this approach, you will always be a step ahead.

RELAXED ON-GUARD POSTURE AGAINST A RIGHT PUNCH

The attacker is in a fighting stance. The defender is in a relaxed on-guard posture. The defender is totally relaxed but aware and alert (1). The opponent attacks with a fast and hard right punch. The defender calmly rolls his shoulder to the right and deflects and intercepts the punch with his right palm (2). The defender quickly shoots a left uppercut to the attacker's jaw. This lifts the attacker's head up to prepare for the next punch in the combination (3). The defender follows through with a backfist to the jaw. Momentum is generated for the backfist by simultaneously stepping forward with the right leg and striking. This enhances the *chi* factor in striking (4). By maintaining continuous flow, the defender concludes the combination with a left punch to the attacker's chest. The right foot plays an important role in this punch. To utilize the maximum chi power, the defender stays relaxed as he simultaneously punches and slides his right foot back to increase the chi factor (5).

RELAXED ON-GUARD POSTURE AGAINST A KICK

The attacker prepares to kick, while the defender is in a relaxed on-guard posture (1). The attacker launches a hard front kick, and the defender defuses the power of the kick by simultaneously deflecting it with his left hand and sliding his right foot back as he moves slightly to his right (2). Remember, all lateral movements can defuse a straight attack regardless of the power. The defender explodes with an open-hand counter to set up the next punch (3). The defender continues the flow of the combination, drops down and then executes a right punch to the attacker's solar plexus (4). The dropping-down motion is another way of maximizing the *chi* factor.

When striking to the body, dropping down will add to chi power. Also, rising up and striking to the head will add momentum to chi power. Those of you who are boxing fans will remember the second fight between Floyd Patterson and Ingemar Johansson. Johansson was knocked out cold when Patterson "dipped" his body and sprung up with a left hook that landed square on Johansson's jaw. One boxing writer called Patterson's punch "the kangaroo punch." Johansson was out cold for a good five to 10 minutes, with his foot quivering uncontrollably. The act of dipping and rising is one of the ways to increase the chi factor in striking.

DEFENSE AGAINST ATTACKS FROM VARIOUS ANGLES

In this section, I will attempt to demonstrate some of the defensive angles to help you avoid getting hit. Again, the key to developing an airtight defense is to blend with your opponent's attack, or to use an old cliché, you want to "roll with the punches." In my own repertoire of defensive moves, I have condensed defense to these basic movements: the parry, the deflection, the roll, the slip, the duck, the cross-block and the weave. The relaxed-focus factor dictates the choice of these defensive moves. When you choose to respond to a hard attack with softness, the best moves are those that enhance harmonization. This is why attitude will help you determine the approach.

In the parry, you redirect your opponent's energy away from you by slightly turning his wrist as you step backward. Whether you redirect it laterally to your left or to your right depends on the opponent's attack hand.

THE PARRY

The attacker throws a body punch, but the defender executes an inside parry as he steps back and slightly to the side.

Deflecting an attack will help you avoid taking the blunt of an opponent's power. The defender must move in the direction of the power yet slightly away from the attack. The entire body must be in a state of relaxed tension. When I talk about relaxed tension, I am not talking about tightness. The kind of tension utilized in relaxed tension is more like a flexible spring that gives but is able to recoil with whipping power. Even though the deflection is in a defensive mode, it is in a position to explode with penetrating counter-power. The deflection is executed inside an opponent's blow or outside his attacking arm.

THE DEFLECTION

The attacker throws a straight right punch, but the defender executes an outside deflection. From this position, the defender can use the deflecting hand to immobilize the attacker's arm and continue with a variety of counters (1). The attacker throws a left punch, but the defender deflects the punch with an inside deflection (2).

OUTSIDE DEFLECTION AND ARM IMMOBILIZATION

The attacker attempts a right punch. The defender slides to his left and deflects the punch with the back of his right hand (1). Once the punch has been deflected and before the attacker withdraws his arm, the defender grasps the attacker's wrist to immobilize it and counterattack (2). Once the attacker's arm is immobilized, the defender completes his counter by striking the nerve on the attacker's forearm to set up for the finishing punch (3). The defender completes his counterattack with a right hammerfist to the attacker's jaw (4).

One of the great masters of the roll in boxing is James "Lights Out" Toney. In his prime, Toney could just roll his shoulder, causing his opponent's punch to whiz past him harmlessly and open the opponent up to a vicious counterattack. The roll works best when the defender is completely relaxed without anticipation or tension. The move must be effortless and fluid.

THE OUTSIDE ROLL

The attacker throws a left punch and the defender rolls his shoulder to his right, making the attacker miss (1). Once the roll is completed and the opponent misses his punch, the defender traps the attacker's arm for a follow-through finishing punch (2). The defender completes his counterattack with a punch to the attacker's ribs (3).

THE INSIDE ROLL

The attacker throws a straight left jab, but the defender rolls his right shoulder and deflects with the left palm (1). When the opponent attacks with a right punch, the defender rolls the left shoulder and deflects with the right palm (2).

More ways to defend are slipping, ducking and weaving. In the structure of the soft approach to power attacks, slipping, ducking and weaving neutralize the attacker's power by making him miss. No matter how powerful an attack, responding by moving away from the attack can be quite unsettling to the attacker when he suddenly realizes that there is no target and only empty space. Slipping, ducking and weaving are an integral part of a Western boxer's defensive arsenal. This is why a boxing coach or trainer places so much emphasis on head-and-body movement. The slipping, ducking and weaving structure compliments the yielding and relaxed-tension modality. In order to effectively implement them, the practitioner must be completely relaxed. Tension impedes flow and fluidity, both of which are necessary ingredients to make slipping, ducking and weaving effective.

The photos will demonstrate the dynamics of each defensive approach in the context of an attack.

THE SLIP

The attacker and the defender (right) are in an on-guard position. The defender is completely relaxed and ready to respond to any attack (1). The attacker executes a hard right punch. The defender slips his body to the left and lets the punch pass by harmlessly. This causes the attacker to stretch out of position (2). As the attacker's punch passes by harmlessly, the defender counters with a right punch to the attacker's rib cage before the attacker is able to retract his missed punch (3).

The difference between a duck and a slip is in the position of the body. In the slip, the body merely slides to the right or left and lets the attacking punch slip past the head over the shoulder. In the duck, the defender drops down under the attacker's strikes.

THE DUCK

The attacker (left) prepares to attack. The defender is in a ready position (1). The moment the attacker punches, the defender drops under the punch, causing the attacker to miss. This leaves the attacker in a vulnerable position for the defender to counterattack (2).

In the weave, the defender moves his upper body left to right and right to left in a bobbing motion. The weave utilizes a little of the slip and a little of the duck—much like a cork bobbing in a tub of water. Often in boxing, people refer to this defensive maneuver as "bobbing and weaving." A weaving fighter can be a tough target to hit. Frazier is a good example of a fighter who utilized the bob-and-weave approach.

THE WEAVE

The attacker and the defender (left) are in on-guard positions. The defender is relaxed, alert and aware to intercept any attack (1). The moment the attacker punches with a left jab, the defender weaves away from the path of the punch (2). Even though the attacker followed through with a right punch after the jab, the defender is able to weave to his right, causing the attacker to miss (3). This leaves the attacker vulnerable to a counterattack.

The cross-block is an appropriate response to a wide punching attack. Although people refer to the cross-block as a "block," it is most effective when you do not try to meet force with force. Rather, you want to help your opponent go in the direction in which the blow is traveling. In other words, yield to the force of the blow. The following photos demonstrate the progression of the cross-block from beginning to completion.

THE CROSS-BLOCK

The defender (right) and attacker are in an on-guard positions (1). The attacker throws a straight right punch. The defender shifts by pivoting on his right foot and executing a cross-block (2). In shifting and pivoting, the defender is helping the power of the attacker's blow dissipate. The defender keeps control of the attacker's arm by helping him continue his downward motion, making a full circle (3). The defender continues the momentum of the circle and pushes the attacker off-balance while stretching his arm and back (4). The defender quickly executes an uppercut to the attacker's ribs while at the same time using his right hand to immobilize the attacker's right arm (5).

As we bring this chapter on dissolving the tools to a close, it is valuable to remember that the highest form of combat is the ability to take techniques from your martial arts repertoire without deliberation. You want to compose combinations effectively as the changing situation requires, much like a composer of music or a prolific writer can take the notes in a scale or letters of the alphabet and turn it into a masterpiece.

To work from this level, you must master each stage of development, from the very basic techniques to the most complicated. Whenever the great coach Vince Lombardi lost a football game, he would require his players to go back to the basics. He knew the basics are where the foundation of the game is, and when you forget the basics, you are competing on shaky foundation. It is no different in martial arts. In order to dissolve the tools, you must be well-grounded in the basics.

CHAPTER FIVE

STAGE FOUR: EXPRESSING THE TOOLS

Expressing the tools is the fourth stage of martial arts development. It is the stage every serious martial artist strives to reach. In the fourth stage, the practitioner moves from deliberation, orchestration and pre-arrangement to one of spontaneous expression. Expressing the tools is working from the "Zen zone" in which reflex action is in harmony with unexpected situations. The defensive art of ducking, slipping and weaving, as discussed in the previous chapter, is a good example of being in the Zen zone in which a reflex action is required to respond to an attack.

Spontaneous response to attacks requires developing the tools in each stage of the process. Professional boxers are great examples of athletes who have mastered the art of expression. Lee was highly critical of those who depended solely on kata training to sharpen their fighting skills. He referred to kata training as "dry-land swimming." Many traditionalists were offended by Lee's comments, while many others considered it seriously and made efforts to change their training regiment. Free sparring is one of the best ways to test your expression skills in fighting. There are a variety of drills that can help you achieve the maximum free-fighting skills. However, the inner substance that is needed to attain sharp free-fighting skills is the ability to maintain a state of relaxed tension, assuming you have developed the tools needed. The essence of fighting skills is based on emotional control, a creative mind and an adaptable spirit. I say adaptable spirit because, in free fighting, the situation is always changing. Unless the fighter is able to adapt to those unexpected quick changes, he will surely be defeated. The quick reflex action needed is really "hair-trigger timing." The spirit must be ready to change and "pull the trigger" without hesitation.

FIGHTING IS A FORM OF COMMUNICATION

When a person reaches the fourth stage of development, it is no longer about techniques as much as it is about intangible attributes. One of those intangible or spiritual qualities is the ability to see combat as a form of communication. I have learned that there are at least six people in a conversation between two. What each says represents two people, what each understands of the other represents another two and what each meant to say but did not represents still two more. Combat is a form of communication in that each communicator must listen to see what the other is about to say. Too many fighters do not bother to listen and observe. Many follow the old adage, "The best defense is a good offense." One of the principles of yielding is to listen and be aware of your opponent's intention and initial move. In life, if you do not listen, there is little interaction; all you have is a monologue. To gain a competitive edge over an opponent, you need to listen to what he is about to say, figuratively and literally. It is in listening that the defender is able to blend into an opponent's sphere.

STAYING IN THE MOMENT

Someone said, "There are two days I never worry about; I hold these two days sacred. The first day is yesterday and the second day is tomorrow." That is a great point to consider when you are in the combat zone; stay in the moment. What you accomplished or didn't in the past is insignificant. Tomorrow, a moment that has not come is of little value in this moment. When I was younger, I did full-contact free sparring three times a week with three different sparring partners. Most of the time, I was able to evade and elude their attacks and counters. Occasionally, I would get hit, sometimes hard. Every time I got hit, I would pause and reflect on why I got hit. Each time I got hit, it was because my mind was not "in the moment." I was thinking about what I did yesterday or I was thinking about how to set my sparring partner up for a hit. I noticed, as long as I stayed in the moment, I could see every initial move by my opponent. I was mentally a step ahead of my sparring partner. I learned that keeping my mind in neutral and in an emotional calm was very effective.

Expressing skills in combat requires a steady, unruffled emotion. When a fighter stays in the moment, his mind is not cluttered with doubts, fears and apprehensions. An analytical mind has its place in developing fighting skills but not while free fighting. This is why staying in the moment is so important. Staying in the moment helps you remain focused and sensitive to your opponent's intention. Staying in the moment enables you to be "free of emotional baggage." Keeping it simple makes the "path" between you and your opponent more direct.

ADAPTING TO THE SITUATION AT HAND

Being able to adapt to a constantly changing situation is the quality of a champion. If there is one thing that gives you the edge, it is being adaptable. Nothing breaks the body and spirit quicker than rigidity. When you reach the "expression stage" of development, the focus should be on "going with the flow" and "blending with your opponent's movements." The chameleon effect definitely gives a fighter a distinct advantage. A great example of the importance of adapting skills was the proposed 2008 Mixed Martial Arts match between Ken Shamrock and Kimbo Slice, aka Kevin Ferguson. Slice studied tapes of Shamrock and trained to take advantage of Shamrock's weaknesses. At the last minute, Shamrock suffered an injury and had to pull out of the bout. The promoter brought in a substitute. Many did not believe that Seth Petruzelli would provide much opposition to the hard-hitting Slice. Petruzelli shocked the MMA world by knocking out Slice in the first round. What happened? Slice lacked the skill to adapt. He had been programmed to fight Shamrock. When you reach the fourth stage of development, fighting should be about adapting and expressing techniques spontaneously. It is about expecting the unexpected. Every expression is done without prearrangement or planned orchestration.

EXPRESSION IN THREE AREAS OF FIGHTING

In this chapter, there are three basic areas of combat: cinematic fighting as in movies, street fighting as in self-defense, and fighting in competition. Even in competition, there are three areas: form competition, point freestyle fighting and full contact. A well-rounded martial artist is able to make the transition smoothly from cinematic, if he or she is into acting, to street fighting to the arena of competition. I believe that the basic foundation does not distinguish one from the other. When it happens, whether it be unexpectedly in a self-defense situation or expectedly on a movie set or in competition, a well-rounded martial artist will be able to express his or her techniques spontaneously. Spontaneity is an inner skill. Expression of techniques spontaneously comes from repetitious practice. The common denominator in proficiency of execution is relaxed tension and relaxed awareness. The more relaxed and focused the practitioner is, the better the timing. Timing is everything.

The following photos demonstrate the same technique utilized under three different circumstances: cinema, self-defense and in competition.

Cinematic fighting is make-believe. In order to give the viewer the illusion that the recipient of the punch was actually hit, camera angle is important. The one who is executing the punch must be relaxed and mentally focused. The puncher must inject emotional content or feeling into the blow. The receiver or the stunt person must have exact timing. The reaction to the blow must be precise. The distance factor is different than actual combat. The two subjects can be several inches apart and the blow can be a total miss, but the reaction of the receiver must be timed to be in sync with the puncher. The stunt person cannot be stiff or tense; he or she must be totally relaxed. The objective in cinematic fighting is to convince the audience that the actor has been hit. Believability is the key.

CINEMATIC FIGHTING: LEFT HOOK

The two actors are facing each other in on-guard postures. Both are relaxed and ready (1). The actor on the right telegraphs his intention by stepping forward as he extends his punching arm (2). In cinematic fighting, it is important to telegraph the techniques to let the viewer know that something is going to happen, but in self-defense or competition, you practice to be nontelegraphic. Notice how the stuntman snapped his head to his left as the blow passed his face. There is distance between the blow and the stuntman's head (3).

CINEMATIC FIGHTING: SIDE KICK

The actors are facing off in on-guard postures. The actor on the right moves forward to reveal his intention that an attack is imminent (1). The actor on the right executes the side kick. The actor on the left must react to the kick by jerking his body in the direction of the kick to make the audience believe that the kick has knocked the wind out of him (2).

CINEMATIC FIGHTING: REVERSE CRESCENT KICK

The actors are moving around in a relaxed on-guard posture. The actor on the left moves to his left on purpose to set up the reverse crescent kick (1). The actor on the right executes the reverse crescent kick, and the actor on the left reacts by snapping his head to his right in the direction of the kick (2).

There are two factors that separate the cinematic fighting and self-defense fighting. In cinematic fighting, the intention is to make the audience believe that the punch or the kick is real and has made contact with the person receiving the blow or kick. In self-defense, the attacker's intention is to hurt the defender, and the defender's goal is to defend and immobilize the attacker, even if the defender must incapacitate the attacker. The other factor is that in cinematic fighting, the one who is attacking must exercise control without physical contact. In self-defense, the attacker's intention is to make full contact with the defender, and the defender will do likewise.

In a life-or-death situation, the defender's attitude can often determine the outcome of an attack. The ability to remain calm and levelheaded will give the defender a winning edge. Anger and fear can impede the ability to express techniques that have been rehearsed and practiced. The following photos demonstrate three techniques that can be used in a self-defense situation: the left hook, the side kick and the reverse crescent kick.

SELF-DEFENSE: LEFT HOOK

The attacker on the left is in an on-guard position. He is prepared to make an initial attack. The defender on the right is in a relaxed on-guard stance. The defender's eyes are focused on the attacker's chest. He is relaxed and ready to hit the attacker on the attacker's initial move (1). The attacker makes his initial move with his left hand. The defender begins countering with a left hook punch (2). The defender lands the left hook on the attacker's jaw (3). The punch can also be targeted to the back of the jaw directly under the ear. Both targets are vulnerable pressure points and are knockout points.

SELF-DEFENSE: SIDE KICK

As the attacker on the left advances toward the defender, the defender turns his body and jams the side kick into the attacker's lower rib cage (1). The key to generating power in the side kick comes from being loose, relaxed and flexible. It is probably the most powerful kick in the kicking arsenal. As the attacker advances toward the defender, the defender drops his side kick to the attacker's knee (2). The knee kick is one of the best weapons in self-defense.

SELF-DEFENSE: REVERSE CRESCENT KICK

The defender fakes a low kick (1). When his opponent reacts, he executes a high reverse crescent kick to the head (2). Note that there are two schools of thought when it comes to using kicks in self-defense. The first is that kicking high can be dangerous, especially if the ground is not stable. The other is that it should be used as a secondary weapon, which I agree with. I believe in setting up kicks with hand techniques.

When people refer to using punches and kicks in competition, they must keep in mind that there are two areas of competition: full-contact tournaments and point tournaments in which light contact is permitted. For example, in full-contact sparring, the left hook is a knockout punch. In point tournaments, the left hook is slightly modified by using the open-hand edge of the thumb part of the hand; this is called a ridgehand strike.

There is little difference between self-defense and competition. In self-defense, kicks and strikes are projected into an intended target, but in competition, a degree of control is encouraged. The object of competition is not to break ribs but to score points. Even in full-contact competition, the objective is to score a knockout rather than disable the opponent, which is the goal of street self-defense.

COMPETITION: LEFT HOOK

The defender and attacker are both in on-guard stances. The defender on the right is relaxed and focused (1). The defender initiates the attack by dipping his knees slightly and executes the left hook (2). The defender completes the left hook to the attacker's temple (3).

COMPETITION: SIDE KICK

The attacker turns his body and executes the side kick to the defender's stomach. The turn and kick is executed simultaneously and not in two movements.

COMPETITION: REVERSE CRESCENT KICK

Kicking can be very effective, especially in light-contact point tournaments. In the same photo used for self-defense on page 85, the kick can be adjusted to tournament competition. The kicker has to exercise control and stop the kick short of full contact. But he has to kick convincingly so if the kick penetrated deeper it would be a "killing" kick.

Whether it be cinematic fighting, self-defense or competition fighting, all three ranges have one thing in common: relaxed tension. To make the techniques work effectively, the person who is delivering them must be relaxed and focused. Hard and stiff tension impedes speed, snap and accuracy.

Another common thread between cinematic, self-defense and competition is doing the techniques versus being the techniques. Only when you can be the techniques will there be depth in what we do. One of the keys to this is the degree in which you have control over your emotions. This is why in the acting profession it's called "emoting." An actor is convincing only when he or she becomes the character for that moment, otherwise he or she is just mouthing the words. It is no different when it comes to kicking, punching and grappling. The entire process must be one of expression. The degree of effectiveness relies on the relaxation factor. Tension will impede flow and fluidity.

No other factor is more important in self-defense situations than maintaining relaxed focus. The need to remain relaxed is important in successfully defending against grappling, hitting and kicking. Once you become tense, you have affected your timing and anxiousness sets in. The following photos will demonstrate some of the ways to handle an attack. In each case, it is important that the defender maintains relaxed tension.

SELF-DEFENSE: SIMPLE ARM GRAB

The attacker grabs the defender's arm (1). Most grab victims will try to pull away, but if you utilize a relaxed-tension approach, you go with the attacker's pull as demonstrated in the following photo. The defender chooses to go with the attacker's pull by pivoting to the left and counterattacking with an elbow (2).

SELF-DEFENSE: DOUBLE WRIST GRAB

The attacker tries to immobilize the defender's arms by grabbing both wrists. The natural response is to try to pull away. Often the strength of the attacker will prevent a successful breakaway (1). The defender demonstrates how you can turn an attack to your advantage by yielding to the attacker's strength. In this case, the defender merely steps forward in the direction of the pull and makes a semicircle with his hands to break free. This leaves the defender in a position to counterattack (2).

RELAXED TENSION IN GRAPPLING DEFENSE

With the advent of mixed martial arts, many of the practitioners use techniques that can cause permanent injuries. There are no specific techniques that will guarantee that a defender will defeat a skilled MMA fighter. Most MMA fighters are conditioned and strong. Meeting strength with strength will only lead to defeat. However, utilizing the "bull and the matador" concept can render physical power and raw strength impotent. Back in the early 1990s when the Ultimate Fighting Championship made its debut, Brazilian *jiu-jitsu* dominated the tournament, especially against strikers from boxing, muay Thai, *savate* and kickboxing. The key to this dominance was the leg takedown executed by Royce Gracie. Gracie would trade strikes with his opponent, then suddenly drop and take down his opponent. It took several years before other competitors adapted to this technique. When attacked, most defenders would back up, only to find themselves with nowhere to run and eventually tap out from Gracie's chokes.

Although mixed martial arts can be effective with its "everything goes" approach in the hands of a skilled practitioner, there is one concept that can nullify its effectiveness, and that is relaxed tension. By merely moving laterally when attacked, the defender moves away from the direct line of fire. This is demonstrated in the following photo sequences.

YIELDING DEFENSE AGAINST A LEG TAKEDOWN

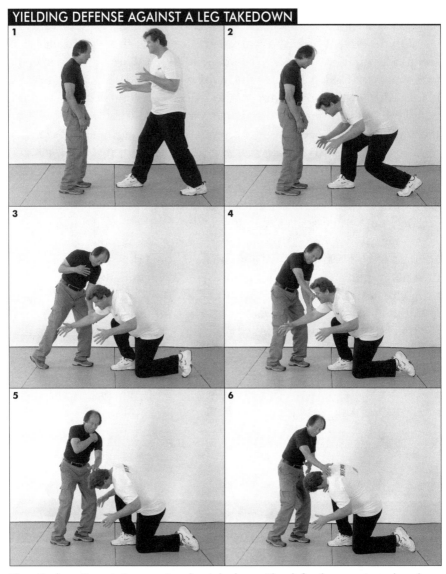

The attacker attempts to execute a leg takedown. The defender remains relaxed, focused and vigilant (1). The attacker drops down for a leg takedown. The defender waits for the attacker to move his arms forward to grab at the defender's legs (2). It is important not to move prematurely. To do so will only negate the defense. As soon as the attacker reaches in for the legs, the defender pivots to the left while at the same time using his own left palm to direct the attacker's arm in the direction of its original intended target (3). Once the defender averts the attacker, the defender counters with a downward open-palm strike to the attacker's nose (4). He follows through by striking the opponent with a open-hand strike to the base of the skull (5-6).

REAR BEAR-HUG DEFENSE

The attacker grabs the defender from the rear (1). As soon as the defender feels the direction of the attacker's strength or energy, he exhales and completely relaxes. He sinks down slightly and grabs the attacker's arms (2). Then the defender spins to his right, causing the opponent to lose balance. From this point, the defender can break free by bringing his left elbow up to strike the defender under the chin (3).

FRONT BEAR-HUG DEFENSE

The attacker grabs the defender (1). The defender must let the body be completely relaxed so he can sink down and lift the attacker's arms up (2). After lifting the attacker's arms up, the defender pivots back and to the side in order to execute a left hook (3).

FRONT BEAR-HUG DEFENSE

In this sequence, the defender demonstrates how to turn the attacker's momentum against himself. The attacker attempts a front bear hug. The defender yields to the attacker's forward momentum by just letting his entire body become relaxed (1). The defender does not resist the attacker. Instead, he yields and redirects the attacker's momentum by pivoting on his left foot (2). At the same time, he pushes the attacker forward by lifting the attacker's leg and driving him forward (3).

FRONT BEAR-HUG DEFENSE

The attacker attempts a front bear hug. The defender goes completely limp with relaxed tension and just lies on the attacker (1). As he rests his weight on the attacker, the defender feels the direction of his momentum. He lifts up his right arm, and at the same time, pushes the attacker's right arm and executes a right body punch (2-3). The defender follows through from the body punch to a right uppercut in order to complete the combination (4).

RELAXED TENSION AND REAR-CHOKE DEFENSE

The attacker executes a rear choke on the defender (1). Rather than struggling to break free, the defender relaxes his body and turns in the direction of the attacker's pressure to spin out of the choke. This puts him in as a position to counter with a punch to the attacker's ribs (2-3).

The key to beating a grappling attack is to just relax and feel the direction of the opponent's power. By yielding to the direction of the opponent's power, the defender can escape and be in a position to counterattack.

RELAXED TENSION AND HITTING DEFENSE

One of the things that I have learned during my many years in martial arts is what worked in your youth may not work in your later years. In youth, you depend on raw physical strength. In later years, physical strength begins to diminish and you must rely on strategy or "smarts" to evade and elude an attack. I work with many seniors on a daily basis; many feel hopeless in the face of potential attacks. Little do they realize that the physical approach to a physical attack is not the appropriate response when you are a senior citizen. What does work is the art of yielding to the attack and the ability to move laterally.

The aikido approach of blending against a hitting attack is quite effective. To move to the side as the attacker advances will neutralize the power of the attack. Moving laterally does not have to be obvious to your attacker. It can be subtle and effortless. The defender only has to be completely relaxed but aware. This is where developing the inner skill is required. You need to have a clear and decisive mind, disciplined emotional control and a sense of connectedness to your opponent. As I said at the beginning of this chapter, self-defense is a form of communication. Listen to what your opponent is about to "say" and be ready to respond.

RELAXED TENSION IN DEFENSE AND COUNTERS

The following photos demonstrate the relationship between relaxed tension and self-defense. When the defender includes the chi factor in his self-defense structure, the relaxation response must be implemented. Chi (energy) is part of your body structure. When tension is present, the chi flow is impeded. The ability to remain relaxed stimulates the chi flow. To increase your chi flow, you must remain relaxed throughout the defensive and offensive process. When the defender comes in contact with the attacker's arm, the defender must relax and yield to the direction of the attacker's power. This is far different from utilizing a power block in which the defender's purpose is to injure the punching arm of the attacker.

RELAXED TENSION IN A PUNCHING ATTACK

The defender (left) and attacker are in on-guard positions. The defender is completely relaxed, aware and alert to any attack that may be launched in his direction (1). The attacker throws a right punch at the defender, who intercepts the attack with a left deflection by making contact with the attacking arm and yielding to the direction of the punch (2).

YIELDING AGAINST AN OVERHEAD ATTACK

Yielding and relaxed tension are effective in all attacks. The reason this is so effective is that most attacks are linear. The response to a linear attack is lateral direction, moving to the side, much like the "bull and the matador." This approach is also quite effective against an overhead attack. Even though the attack comes from over the head, the attack is still in a linear direction. By stepping to the side and touching the attacker's attacking arm, you don't give him your body as a target—only empty space. The key to success in the entire process is the ability to remain relaxed.

YIELDING AGAINST AN OVERHEARD ATTACK

The defender is in a relaxed-arm-folded posture. He is totally relaxed and quietly aware. The attacker assumes an on-guard posture (1). The attacker raises his arm to attack. The defender remains relaxed until the attacker makes his initial move downward (2). As soon as the attacker commits to the downward motion, the defender slides to his left side and simultaneously touches the attacker's arm in preparation to guide the attacking arm in the direction that it was originally headed (3). The defender guides the attacker's arm downward. From here, the defender can choose to counterattack with punches or a kick (4).

YIELD, TRAP AND COUNTER

In this sequence, the defender utilizes a cross-block to set the attacker up for an arm-immobilization strike. The attacker raises his arm to attack. The defender remains in a relaxed on-guard posture (1). As the attacker makes his downward motion, the defender pivots on his right foot and executes a cross-palm block to help the attacker complete his downward motion (2). The defender adheres to the attacker's arm as he completes the downward motion (3). As the defender completes the attacker's downward motion, the defender makes a complete circle with his right arm. He wraps his right arm around the attacker's right arm to immobilize and then pull the attacker forward (4). With the attacker's right arm trapped, the defender counters with a left hook to the attacker's jaw (5).

YIELDING TO KICKING ATTACKS

Kicks can be powerful and lethal to those who are specialists in the art. However, the power of kicks can be neutralized when the defender deflects and dissolves the center of its power. To do that, the defender must shift laterally as he deflects the forward momentum of the kick. Also, by closing the kicking distance, you take the kick away from its range. Again, moving the body and adhering to the kicking leg can help the defender achieve control for counters and aggressive defense. Relaxed tension can help the defender to accomplish this, whereas tension will impede fluidity of movement.

DEFLECT AND COUNTER AGAINST A FRONT KICK

The attacker (right) positions himself to kick, while the defender faces him in a relaxed on-guard posture (1). As the attacker kicks, the defender slides back slightly and, with a semicircular motion, deflects the kick guiding it slightly away from the intended target (2). Once the deflection is completed and the attacker's leg returns to the floor, the defender closes the gap and delivers a backfist strike (3). The backfist counter is completed (4). The defender sinks down and drops a straight body punch to the attacker's solar plexus (5). The breath is an important component in *chi* striking. The body must remain relaxed at all times, and when striking, there should not be any tension. When the punch reaches its intended target, the defender should utilize the "hah" breath to project the chi.

DEFLECTION AND COUNTER AGAINST WHEEL KICKS

Defending against kicking attacks is no different than defending against a punching attack. Skilled kickers intimidate many defenders. The only difference between kicking and punching is the length of the two limbs and the power quotient. Utilizing lateral movements will negate the length and power advantage. In the following sequence of photos, the defender demonstrates the effectiveness of utilizing relaxed tension and yielding to the opponent's power.

DEFENSE AGAINST A KICKING ATTACK

The defender (left) prepares for an attack with a relaxed on-guard posture (1). After the attacker executes a hook kick, the defender slides his left foot back and redirects the kick away from the intended target (2). As the attacker drops his kicking leg on the floor, he attacks with a left punch, which the defender parries (3). The defender follows through with an uppercut to the attacker's ribs (4).

LEG PARRY AND COUNTER AGAINST A PUNCH KICK

The defender (left) prepares to respond in a relaxed on-guard posture (1). As the attacker kicks, the defender slides to his left to parry the kick (2). The defender remains alert to the opponent's energy shift (3). As the attacker shifts his energy to a right punch, the defender senses the change of angle and traps the attacking arm, waiting for the attacker to withdraw (4). Once the defender feels the opponent's energy change, the defender explodes with a backfist strike (5). When sensitivity and feeling becomes part of the martial arts process, you have the advantage of an advance warning system, which gives the defender a distinct edge.

BODY LANGUAGE—READING YOUR OPPONENT

As we conclude Chapter Five, I would like to summarize briefly the dynamics of body language and the ability to read what the opponent's large and small movements are saying. As a social worker with a background in counseling, one of the techniques I use is body language awareness. When clients come in for counseling, most will be in a state of denial. They will try their best to cover up hurts and pain with various defensive mechanisms. The trick to getting these people to open up and tell what is really on their minds and in their hearts is to ask key questions that will "hit close to home." When those questions are asked, and they are the right questions, the person will shift and react with subtle movements. As a counselor, I pick up on those small shifts. I usually ask, "What was that little twitch about?" or "Why don't you give it a voice? Tell me what it is saying." Eventually, the person will say why the question elicited a reaction. It is no different when facing an opponent, regardless of whether it is in competition or self-defense. To put yourself one step ahead of your adversary, you must learn to read his body language. Most people are telegraphic. They will tell you when and where they will hit if you are keenly aware of unusual movements. Ken Norton, the former world heavyweight boxing champion, broke the great Ali's jaw the second time they met. He picked up on a slight movement that told him when Ali was ready to jab. Norton observed that every time Ali got ready to jab, he would twitch his pectoral muscles. Norton timed the telegraphic movement and punched over the jab, breaking Ali's jaw with a right counter.

A similar incident happened between boxing contender Joe Louis—who was undefeated, winning most of his fights by knockouts—and Max Schmeling, a top 10 boxing contender from Germany in 1937, who later became the world heavyweight champion.

Earlier, Schmeling was in the audience to watch Louis fight another opponent. After the fight, he said to his manager, "I think I saw something." He would not elaborate. When the match was made between Louis and Schemling, he took advantage of what he saw. Although it was just a little thing, it was the key to his knockout of the undefeated Louis. What Schmeling see that night: Every time Louis would jab, he would drop his left hand. Schmeling exploited that mistake. He won by a knockout. Louis took some heavy punishment, especially to the left side of his face where Schmeling had countered him with devastating right crosses.

The ability to read an opponent is the key to winning and controlling the fight. Developing keen awareness is no easy task. It takes a lot of practice to understand the habits of humans. The body also must be in tune to what the other person is saying, verbally and otherwise. When you reach the expression stage in the development process, the internal qualities must be refined. Reading body language is one of those skills that enhance quiet awareness.

CHAPTER SIX

DEVELOPING THE RELAXATION RESPONSE

Looking back, I now realize the limitation of just working on the physical level, and the fight between Jack Dempsey and Gene Tunney illustrates this. Dempsey was a physical fighter. He constantly bore in, bobbing and weaving and punching with dynamite in each fist. His destruction of Jess Willard, who was 6 feet 5 inches tall and weighed 240 pounds, was a great testimony to Dempsey's power. On the other hand, Tunney was just the opposite. He used his mind more than his body. When he was finally matched up with Dempsey, the odds were against him. Yet Tunney managed to beat Dempsey twice by decision. The defining moment for Tunney was in the so-called "long count." When Dempsey knocked down Tunney, Dempsey refused to go to a neutral corner. The referee refused to count until Dempsey went to a neutral corner. It was said that between the time Tunney was knocked down and the count ended, more than 14 seconds had lapsed. What I observed from film footage was that Tunney remained calm and in control while all this was transpiring. He got up and eventually won the match.

In this chapter, I will discuss some of the exercises that I have used to enhance the relaxation-response mode. It is easy to tense up when you are upset, scared, angry, apprehensive or worried. It is the goal of this book and this chapter to help you as a martial artist develop a relaxation response to daily events.

In order for an individual to reach that level of emotional control within the context of martial arts and daily life, the training focus should include internal training that will condition the inner spirit. When I speak of "inner spirit," I am referring to all the intangibles that make you fully functional. Those intangibles are. The emotion, energy flow, attitude and mind or thought process. Of all the internal qualities, your emotions are the most difficult to control.

Years ago, I was counseling a young man who became deeply depressed because his girlfriend had ended their relationship. I suggested to him that he should get involved in some activity that may take his mind off his loss. He said, "No matter what I do, it seems like a dark cloud is hanging over me. Life does not seem to be worth living." That young man is a good example of how emotion can be difficult to control. It takes a lot of training to bring your emotions under control. Many fights have been lost in the heat of battle because the contestants fail to maintain a disciplined emotion. By the same token, when someone cuts in front of you on the freeway, you react with rage. How about choosing to remain calm and keep your emotions in neutral without any stressful reaction? As difficult as it is to control the emotion, it can be done through regular training. Some of the exercises in this chapter will help you do that.

MEDITATION

There are many approaches to meditation. Some are more abstract and complicated than others. What works for me is simply finding a comfortable position in a chair, lying down or standing up. The position is a matter of choice. I prefer to sit in a chair. Sometimes I do it standing up, especially when I train outdoors. In order for meditation to be beneficial, certain conditions must be taken into consideration. Once you have settled into a comfortable position, let your entire body be relaxed. Let go of all the tension. Don't rush. Once your body is completely relaxed, relax your mind and let go of all your thoughts. With your mind and body in a completely relaxed mode, slowly inhale, pause and slowly exhale. Think of nothing. Just let your mind and body be completely relaxed.

There is a saying in regards to meditation: When the body is in motion, the inner self is in stillness. When the body is completely immobile and relaxed, the inner self is in action. Meditation allows the body to remain still so the inner body can kick in. The chi or energy flows freely, blood begins to circulate, emotions are under control and the mind functions on a deeper level, circumventing the mental spasms that clutter the surface. It was said that legendary swordsman Miyamoto Musashi spent most of his days in a cave meditating. It is also interesting to note that he did not have a sparring partner to hone his skills. Musashi sharpened his swordsmanship with meditation. Meditation allowed him to discipline his emotions and sharpen his mental focus. When faced with an adversary, Musashi was not distracted. He mentally and emotionally focused on the challenge at hand. Months and years of meditation had conditioned him to activate his inner skills when needed.

THE SITTING POSITION

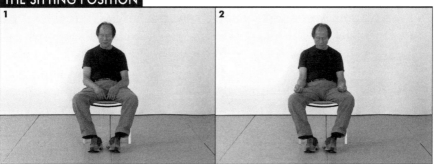

In this position, let the body and mind be completely relaxed. The hands are resting on the thigh, totally relaxed. Keep your eyes closed (1). Meditation is also a discipline for filtering out noises. Meditation is the time to put your selective hearing into gear. Think of nothing, regardless of the thousands of noises around you—just be in the moment. This position is similar to the previous photo. The only difference is the position of the hands. The palms are facing up (2). The hand position is popular with meditation practitioners that utilize the lotus position.

STANDING MEDITATION POSITION

In the standing position, bend the knees slightly and have your palms face each other. The *chi* point of entry and exit is the palm of the hands.

PRONE POSITION OR LYING DOWN POSITION

The prone position is probably the most relaxed position. Many who meditate from this position end up falling asleep. It is important to keep a mental and emotional focus so you don't fall asleep. One of the benefits from meditating is the ability to control insomnia—at least that is true for me. I can turn the "switch" off or on. This ability to control sleep is the results of years of meditating.

When the palms are facing each other, the chi flow is able to interact. In this position, stay relaxed and feel the chi surging throughout the body. The fingers will tingle and the limbs will feel a relaxed heaviness. Relaxed tension "kicks in" and you will feel a sense of relaxed strength.

MEDITATION IN MOTION

In addition to my daily practice of meditation in stillness, I also practice meditating in motion. This exercise allows me to practice maintaining a relaxed focus while in motion. It is similar to *tai chi chuan* because the movements are slow, deliberate and relaxed. As I mentioned earlier in this chapter, when the outer body is in motion, the inner body is in stillness. When the outer body is in stillness, the inner body is in motion. In the following series of exercise, which I practice on a daily basis with light dumbbells, I strive to remain relaxed, even when I speed up the process. One of the paradoxical principles is brought into play, and that principle is: When you want to achieve speed, you train slowly. When you want to control your opponent's power, you yield to the force. The following photos are a series of punching combinations that help me attain several internal qualities. First, it sharpens my punching skills. Second, it helps me develop flow and continuity within. Third, the relaxed motion of moving meditation allows me to strike with speed.

When a punch or a strike is executed in a relaxed state, you remove "tension blocks." These blocks inhibit the free flow of energy that is needed to attack the pressure points of your opponent. Practicing moving meditation helps develops a relaxed-tension state that will enhance free chi flow no matter what the circumstances.

MEDITATION IN MOTION

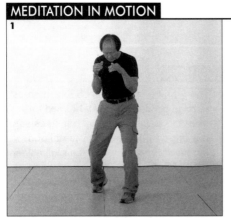

(1) Begin in an on-guard stance. The entire body should be relaxed but ready. In this relaxed state, be aware of the internal activities that are transpiring between your mind, body, emotion and spirit. Slowly execute a left jab. Let the punch flow slowly in front of you. As you retract the left jab, be prepared to step forward with a straight right punch.

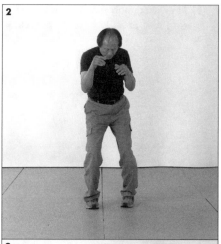

(2) Slowly step forward as you execute the right punch. Every movement should be slow and smooth. Coordinate your breathing with the movement of your body.

(3) Prepare to step forward with your left foot to execute a left hook punch.

(4) Make the transition from the straight right punch to the left hook punch.

Continued ▶

(5) After executing the left hook, step forward and execute a right uppercut.

(6) Remain in the same stance as in the previous photo and execute a right hook off of the right uppercut. A right hook off of a right uppercut is a natural flowing pattern. The key to getting into the flow is to feel the flow from one angle to the next without breaking your inner rhythm. A good analogy is shifting gears in your car. When a car is moving forward, you shift from first gear to second and then to the third, but if you suddenly shift from first to reverse, you're in trouble. You would no doubt strip the gears and ruin your transmission.

(7) Step again with the left foot and execute a left uppercut.

(8) Execute a left uppercut off of a left hook punch.

(9) From the left hook position, slowly step forward with the right foot and execute a reverse hammerfist strike.

(10) From the right reverse hammerfist strike, step forward with the left foot and execute a left reverse hammerfist strike.

Continued ▶

(11) From the left reverse hammerfist strike position, make the transition to a right hammerfist strike by stepping forward with the right foot leading. Please note: There is a difference between a reverse hammerfist and a hammerfist. The reverse hammerfist utilizes the pinkie-finger side of the fist with your palms down, and the target area is the opposite side of your opponent's jaw. The hammerfist utilizes the same side of the fist but with the palm up and aimed at the same side of your opponent's jaw.

(12) From the right hammerfist position, step forward with your left foot and execute a left hammerfist. You automatically return to the starting on-guard position.

This punching sequence gives you, the practitioner, the basic punches needed to advance from the first stage of development to the fourth stage of development. Without good basic techniques, it is difficult to advance to a high level of fighting skills. To reach a professional skill level, you must diligently practice these basic techniques to move from the developing stage, through the refinement stage, and into the dissolving and expression stages. To make those advances, you must continue to practice on a daily basis. The key "vehicle" as you navigate through the stages of development is good basics.

Again, I must reiterate: It is better to master a few techniques well than to know a thousand and master none. The art of yielding and the art of relaxed focus and relaxed tension is not about quantity; it is about depth and inner development. When a martial artist has mastered his techniques from within, he or she is much more effective than a person who has only skimmed the surface.

In moving meditation, remember the Four F's: form, flow, feeling and footwork. Always remain relaxed at all times, regardless of whether you are standing still or moving from one position to the next. Synchronize your breathing with the movements of your hands and feet. Let your entire body feel every move. Be aware, be alert and be alive.

PRAYER

When I mention prayer, most people consider it to be a religious rite or religious practice. Although I am a member of the faith community, I do not look at prayer as a religious rite; I look at prayer as a vehicle to get in touch with my inner self within the context of the God force that is in and around me. To me. the source of energy and personal power comes from this creative force called God. Prayer creates a spiritual environment that helps me control the fear factor and create a relaxed environment. Tension and stress finds its roots in fear, anger, apprehension, anxiety and doubt. When your faith is grounded in the God force and the God spirit, you do not feel like you are facing the world and its challenges alone. You are empowered by God's presence.

Prayer can take shape in many forms. It can be a quiet conversation between you and God. It can be in the form of a feeling of appreciation for all life. Some people look at a beautiful garden and feel a sense of prayer. Others see a beautiful sunset and feel their spirits lifted. Still others find their heart warmed with music. Whatever form, prayer can build confidence and help manage stress and tension. Prayers are a powerful vehicle for stabilizing the emotions and strengthening of the spirit. Prayer is positive self-talk. Prayer is the mind speaking to the heart in the presence of the spirit.

USING PRAYER FOR RELAXATION

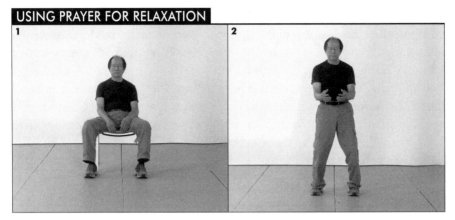

You can pray by sitting down. Much like meditation, the body should remain relaxed, and the focus is on what you really want to happen in your life (1). Prayer allows you to verbalize your wishes and desires. If it is inner peace that you are seeking, prayer is one of the vehicles that can help you achieve it. Prayer can be done standing up. Let the entire body be relaxed and focus on the image of God (2). In this moment, ask for those things that will empower and strengthen your inner self.

The two photos are a sample of some of the many prayer positions you can take. Actually, praying can be done from many venues and positions. It is not confined just to sitting and standing. It can be done while in bed before you sleep. I have said many prayers while traveling by air or sitting at the airport waiting for a flight. Prayer allows me to let go of those elements that cause me to be anxious and tense. If you want to develop a relaxation response to whatever life brings you, prayer can be a very powerful vehicle.

VISUALIZATION

Visualization is the ability to see what you want to happen before it happens. When you can see it in your mind's eye, there is a good chance it can become real in your life. Many top athletes use visualization to enhance their athletic skills. I first became interested in visualization in the early 1960s when I came across an article in *Psychology Today* on how Jean-Claude Killey won the 1968 Winter Olympics in skiing. The entire article was devoted to how Killey used visualization to navigate the difficult twists and turns of the slopes of Squaw Valley in California. He said when he actually began his run, everything he had visualized in his mind's eyes unfolded right before him.

Several years ago, I heard that a research group decided to test the value of visualizing, so they recruited two basketball teams to participate in the experiment. One team would practice shooting free throws, while the other team did nothing physical; they just sat and visualized shooting free throws. When the experiment was over and the two teams went on the floor to shoot free throws, it was said that the team that did the visualization won the contest.

I once read about a man by the name of Harry S. Decamp who was diagnosed with bladder cancer. When he went to the hospital for surgery, they sent him home. His cancer had spread and surgery would have been ineffective. He returned home very depressed. He sat in front of his television looking at the images on the screen but not really paying much attention to the program because he was in a deep depression, knowing he was going to die. He did this day in and day out, just sitting in front of the television and feeling sorry for himself. He had no appetite and was losing weight. One day, a thought came into his mind: Why not imagine in his mind's eye that creatures like Pac-Man are swimming inside of him and eating up his cancer cells? As they ate up the bad cells, his body was replenished with good cells from healthy white and red blood cells. Day and night, Decamp visualized these images in his mind.

One day, Decamp said to his wife, "Honey, would you go down the street and get me a couple of submarine sandwiches?" His wife looked at him with skepticism and said, "Harry, I think you are hallucinating." Harry replied, "No, I really mean it. I am hungry. Go and get me two submarine sandwiches." Still skeptical, his wife went reluctantly and came back with two submarine sandwiches. She laid them on the coffee table and brought him a glass of water. She went into the kitchen to do some chores. When she came back, she said, "Harry, what happened to the sandwiches?" Harry replied, "I ate them!" The wife replied, "What? You ate them?" "Yes, I was hungry," Harry replied. Months later, Harry went to see his doctor. They took an X-ray and found no cancer. The cancer had gone into remission.

What the mind can conceive and believe and act on, you can achieve.

The following photos will illustrate some of the imaging and visualization I do to sharpen my martial arts skills. Using the imagination is an integral part of visualization. Whenever I want to accomplish something, I sit back in a comfortable position in a chair and close my eyes and begin to create visual scenarios in my mind's eyes. The photos demonstrate the content of the mental images you want the mind's eye to see. In the first scenario, I imagine an attacker throwing a left jab.

VISUALIZATION SCENARIO NO. 1

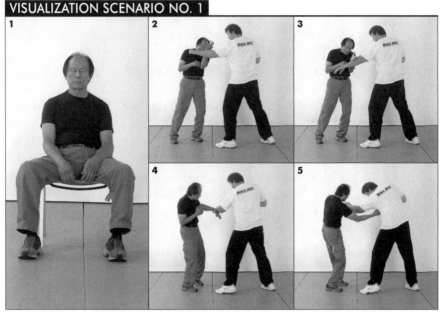

The visualization position is similar to the prayer and meditation positions. It is important to be comfortable and relaxed before activating the imagination (1). I start with the visual sequence of the attacker striking with a left jab, but I cross block with my left hand (2). I continue to sweep the attacker's arm to control his body (3). In this photo, I adhere to the opponent's arm to set him up with the final blow (4). As I stretch the attacker's arm and chest, I counter with a punch to the ribs (5).

These photos are an example of how you can create various combinations to imprint on the mind so that the body will follow when you physically do the movements. The imagination allows you to create a scenario for your opponent. Imagine what he might do to you and how you will respond. Put details into each visualized action. What the mind can conceive, it can achieve.

In the following photos, I have created an imaginary scenario of a leg-takedown defense. As a stand-up fighter, I am very aware of the effectiveness of a leg takedown. Once you are on the ground, you are in the grappler's zone. To minimize the chance of being taken to the ground, you must yield to the attacker's aggressiveness. I first conceived of the leg-takedown defense from watching MMA matches. The question I asked myself, "How can I circumvent the age and size factor in relationship to explosive grappling attacks?" What I came up with is to yield to the opponent's power by going with the flow and moving to the side. When my hand is on the grappler's body, I am able to follow the direction of his energy. By yielding and moving in sync with him, he will never have a chance to take control of the fight. I began to visualize this in my mind's eye and then practiced it in shadow fighting. When I did meet up with someone who specialized in leg takedowns and grappling, I discovered the effectiveness of this defense. Every time he moved, I moved.

VISUALIZATION SCENARIO NO. 2

The attacker is in an on-guard stance. He is positioning himself to go for a leg takedown (1). As the attacker drops down for the leg takedown, I touch one of the attacking arms and slide to the side. At the same time, I parry his arm away from my leg (2). By moving to the side and lightly touching and parrying the attacker's extended arm, I give the attacker only empty space. I continue to lead the attacker's energy forward, causing him to lose balance and become vulnerable to a counterattack (3). In order for this process to work, I must use relaxed tension.

VISUALIZATION SCENARIO NO. 3

The attacker and I are in on-guard postures. The attacker fakes a right punch and is ready to drop down and go for the defender's legs (1). As the attacker attempts a leg takedown, I put both hands lightly on the attacker's shoulders and guide him forward while sliding back. When the attacker moves, I move. If the attacker tries to shift, I will shift with him (2-3).

The key to visualization is in the defender maintaining relaxed tension. All attacks can be neutralized when the defender maintains a relaxed-tension, relaxed-focus mind-set. Get into your opponent's rhythm and move when he moves, shift when he shifts, and dissolve and deflect when he attacks. When you become one with your opponent, you have minimized his target for attack. What you strive to do in the art of yielding is to put him in a position of fighting himself. Every time he moves, he is giving out signals as to what he is going to do and when. By blending in, you take control.

CHI BREATHING

What is the difference between regular breathing and chi breathing? In regular or natural breathing, the involuntary muscles come into play. As long as you are alive, you automatically breathe. Most of the breathing is surface or chest breathing. In chi breathing, the breath is deep and long. You consciously try to breathe all the way down to your navel, or as Chinese health professionals call it, you breathe *"dan tien"*—three inches from the navel. The breath should be a slow four-count inhale and a slow four-count exhale.

In addition to the slow four-count deep breathing, there is also the "hah" breath. The "hah" breath is correctly done when you inhale, pause and expel the air from the bottom of your abdomen as if you are a balloon that has just been deflated. You exhale with the sound of "hah." The body should be completely relaxed. The breath is very important in chi striking. Utilizing the "hah" breath when striking can add tremendous impact to your punches. In physical punching, the power is generated by throwing the entire body into the punch, whereas in chi punching you "hah" at the point of contact and let your entire body go limp as you project the chi through the target.

The following photos will help develop your breathing and expand lung capacity.

CHI-BREATHING EXERCISE NO. 1

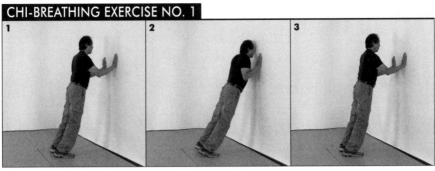

Place both hands on the wall. Let your entire body relax (1). Slowly inhale as you lower your body. Pause and hold your breath (2). Slowly exhale as you return to the starting position (3). Make all inhales and exhales slow and on a four count. Do this first sequence 10 times.

In the second sequence, exhale as you push against the wall. Start by taking a deep breath.

CHI-BREATHING EXERCISE NO. 2

This time, you will exhale as you push against the wall. Start by taking a deep breath. Exhale slowly (four counts) as you lower your body. Pause and slowly inhale as you return to the starting position (1-2).

CHI-BREATHING EXERCISE NO. 3

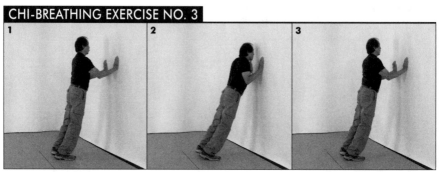

Slowly inhale and fill the lungs as you lower your body (1-2). Slowly return to the starting position. Hold your breath, keep the body relaxed and repeat for 10 repetitions. Exhale and inhale on the fifth repetition (3).

CHI CIRCULATION EXERCISES

The series of exercises in this section is designed to enhance your relaxation response. A totally relaxed body is necessary to reap the maximum benefit from these chi circulation exercises.

TWIST AND SWING

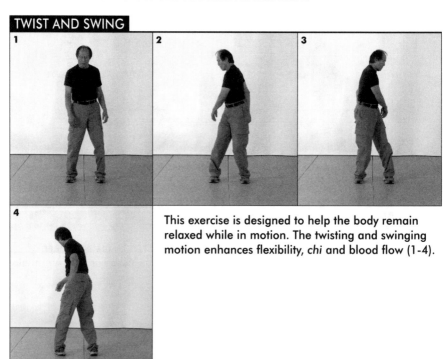

This exercise is designed to help the body remain relaxed while in motion. The twisting and swinging motion enhances flexibility, *chi* and blood flow (1-4).

BACK-AND-SHOULDER TAP

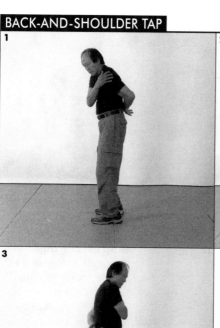

The second series of *chi* circulation exercises is the back-and-shoulder tap. Keep the body relaxed and loose. Swing left and right. As you swing, tap your back with one arm and tap your shoulder with the other palm. By remaining relaxed, you will active the chi flow (1-3).

CIRCLE AND BREATHE

Continue to remain totally relaxed. Slowly inhale and bring your arms upward, making a big circle. As you complete the circle, slowly inhale as you return to the start position. Repeat the process for a 10 count (1-3).

ARM SWING AND EXPEL THE BREATH

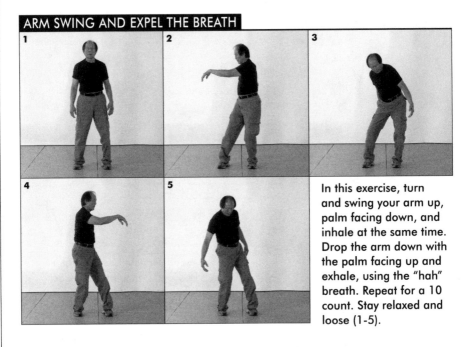

In this exercise, turn and swing your arm up, palm facing down, and inhale at the same time. Drop the arm down with the palm facing up and exhale, using the "hah" breath. Repeat for a 10 count. Stay relaxed and loose (1-5).

SCOOP UP THE ENERGY AND EXPEL THE STRESS

Begin in a relaxed standing position. Inhale as you simulate a scooping motion, crossing your hands at the same time (1-2). Pause slightly at the top and drop your hands, as if you are wringing out the stress, and exhale (3). Repeat for a count of 10 (4-5). Remain relaxed and loose throughout the entire process.

The information in this chapter on developing the relaxation response is divided into four components: meditation, prayer, visualization and chi breathing. The scope of the entire program is not implemented separately in practice. Rather, the four components are practiced as one unit. When you sit down to meditate, you also approach this moment as a prayer. While in the prayer/meditation mode, you visualize the results and at the same time focus on slow, deep chi breathing.

To develop a relaxation-response approach to life and martial arts, you must practice all the elements that will enhance a relaxed-focus, relaxed-tension and a relaxed-awareness mind-set. In order to condition your physical and internal being to remain relaxed in all situations, you must practice the relaxation response every moment of the day, no matter how stressful some events may seem. I look at my daily world, from the busy freeway to Starbucks, as a training ground for developing the relaxation response. When an irate driver gives you the "bird," you have the choice of remaining emotionally neutral or going into a rage. When someone breaks into the line at Starbucks, you can calmly remind the person that the line forms back there or you can become so angry that the situation escalates into a physical confrontation. Practicing relaxation responses in all of life begins with a personal choice. As you continue to repeat the same choice, relaxation responses become a conditioned response. I think I am a great testimony of this. In my younger days, it did not take much to push my combat button. In later years, it takes a lot to get me mad. After practicing the relaxation response for more than 15 years, I think the peaceful warrior mind-set has become ingrained into my psyche.

CHAPTER SEVEN

CHI POWER THROUGH WEIGHT TRAINING

In 1954, I moved West from Widener, Arkansas, to serve a United Methodist Church in Sacramento, California. While driving down P Street in Sacramento, I happened to glance over to see a monster of a man standing in front of a building that was being renovated. I stepped on the brakes, backed up and parked. As I walked up the street toward this man with the build of Paul Bunyan, I realized it was Bill Pearl, former Mr. America and two-time Mr. Universe. His arms were bulging out of his form-fitting T-shirt. It seemed as if his entire body was screaming to get out of that shirt, which was stretched to its limit. I didn't know whether I should go up to him and greet him or just turn and walk away. Before I could decide, he walked up to me, extended his hand and said, "Hi, I am Bill Pearl. I am opening up a gym here and invite you to come and workout." I knew nothing about weight training. I spent most of my life and athletic career running, doing push-ups, chin-ups and sit-ups. My boxing coach had forbidden me from doing any type of weight training. He believed that heavy-resistance exercises made you muscle-bound and slow. But when I met Pearl, I was fascinated. Three days later when he had his grand opening, I was there to watch demonstrations of posing and lifting. I was hooked and signed up immediately. I learned a lot from Pearl about weight training. I practiced all the exercises he taught me. I followed his program faithfully three to four times a week until I suffered a serious injury to my shoulders in 1994. When I injured my shoulder, I no longer could lift heavy weights. It was here that my injury and inability to lift heavy poundage was my inspiration for developing *chi fung.*

I began to experiment with the circular motions I had learned in kung fu with light dumbbells while implementing the principles of tai chi chuan and *qigong*, both of which rely on slow-motion movements, a relaxed focus and slow, deep breathing in sync with movements of exercise. What resulted in this approach were not bulky and big muscles, but a body that felt powerful in relaxation or a relaxed-tension state of being. I also noticed in my martial arts that I was not as tense when executing techniques. Rather, I enjoyed a greater flow and fluidity. Movements, such as punching and kicking, were more effortless. I was trying hard without trying. It was an amazing transformation from taking the hard-and-heavy approach to a soft and more yielding posture. The true essence of yielding and relaxed tension is found in the inner core where the chi flows and circulates. Using the principles of tai chi and qigong with weight training seems to accelerate the chi flow. The following exercises are some of the movements I have developed in chi fung. They are my favorite. Each exercise is designed to target at least one body part. However, the movements will also affect related muscles. For example, when you do a chest lateral, which affects the pectoral muscles in the chest, the exercise will also affect the shoulders or deltoid muscles. When one group of muscles is targeted, several other groups will benefit. This is another aspect about chi fung: It develops functional muscles rather than lifting muscles. Functional muscles are multidimensional, whereas lifting muscles are much stronger when it comes to lifting but are one dimensional.

To get the maximum benefit from the practice of the following chi-based exercises, remember the acronym RSVP: relax, slow motion, visualize and pause.

The bottom line: Take your time and be aware of all the inner dynamics that occur during the movements. Start with a light dumbbell (between 3 pounds to 8 pounds). If that's too light, add on more weights, but not so much that it will direct your entire focus on lifting. The poundage should be enough to give resistance to the muscles and, at the same time, allow you to focus on breathing, visualizing and pausing as you lower the weights. The balance between external and internal activities promotes a state of relaxed tension.

CHI EXERCISE NO. 1

(1) In this first exercise in the *chi fung* series, the focus is on the pectoral or chest muscles, although the collateral effects will impact the shoulders, arms and triceps. Begin by standing relaxed with the weight hanging from the side. Take a slow, deep breath and a slow, long exhale.

(2-3) Slowly inhale as you curl the weights to the chest. Slight pause.

(4-5) Make a semi-circle, with the left hand in a clockwise direction and the right hand in a counterclockwise direction. Exhale slowly as the fists face each other, with elbows lifted.

(6-7) Make a reverse semicircle, much like executing a double uppercut. Move the left fist in a counterclockwise direction and the right fist in a clockwise direction. Slowly inhale as you execute the movements.

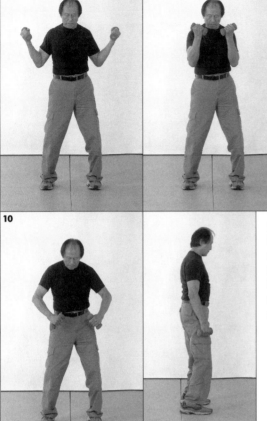

(8-9) Hold your breath while stretching your pectoral muscles. Pause as you return to the chest position.

(10) Slowly exhale as you lower the weights and return to the starting position. Relax and release all the tension in your body. Repeat the process again until you have completed 10 repetitions.

CHI EXERCISE NO. 2

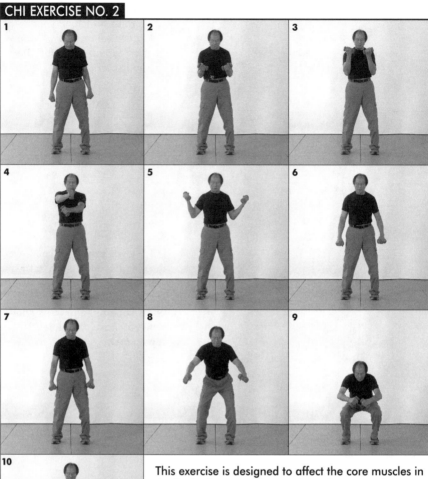

This exercise is designed to affect the core muscles in the body. Core muscles are those ligaments that provide strength to the joints. Unlike the exterior muscles, the core muscles are the inner muscles that provide strength for lifting, hitting, kicking and other activities. Stand relaxed with the weights to your side (1). Exhale and let your entire body relax. Slowly inhale as you curl the weights up to your chest (2-3). Pause slightly and slowly exhale as you extend your arms (right arm over the left) (4). Pause. Slowly inhale as you stretch your arms outwardly (5). Pause and slowly exhale as you lower the weights back to the starting position (6). From the starting position, inhale as you slowly squat as if you were hugging a tree (7-9). Pause. Slowly stand back up and exhale and relax as you return to the starting position (10). Repeat the movement, and as you bring the weights up to your chest, pause and cross your left arms over the right and exhale. Repeat the entire process for 10 repetitions.

CHI EXERCISE NO. 3

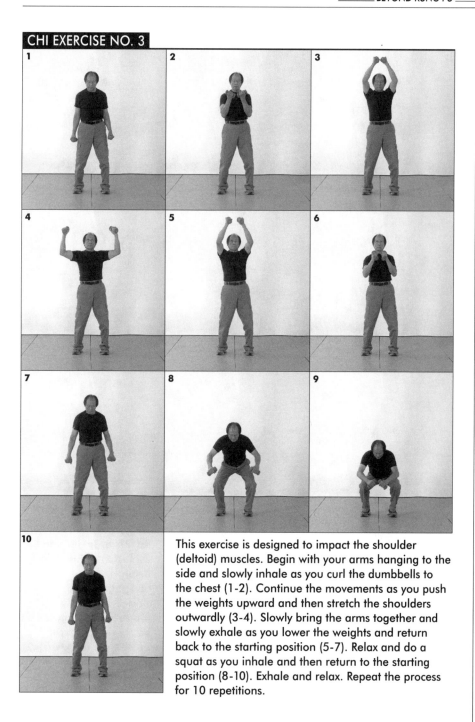

This exercise is designed to impact the shoulder (deltoid) muscles. Begin with your arms hanging to the side and slowly inhale as you curl the dumbbells to the chest (1-2). Continue the movements as you push the weights upward and then stretch the shoulders outwardly (3-4). Slowly bring the arms together and slowly exhale as you lower the weights and return back to the starting position (5-7). Relax and do a squat as you inhale and then return to the starting position (8-10). Exhale and relax. Repeat the process for 10 repetitions.

CHI EXERCISE NO. 4

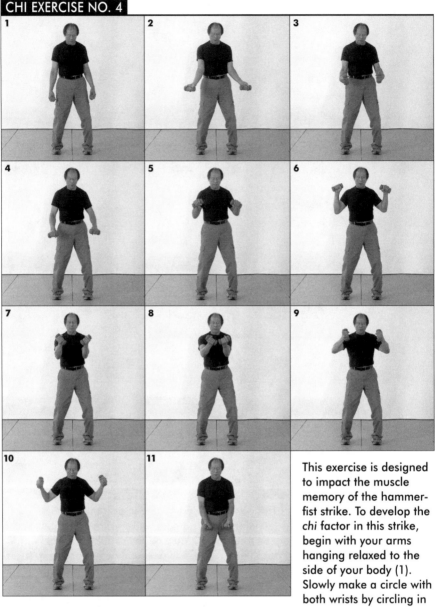

This exercise is designed to impact the muscle memory of the hammer-fist strike. To develop the *chi* factor in this strike, begin with your arms hanging relaxed to the side of your body (1). Slowly make a circle with both wrists by circling in a clockwise direction with the left wrist and counterclockwise with the right wrist (2). Make the circles for a three count, with your palms facing down (3-4). Slowly inhale as you raise the weights to shoulder height, pause and slowly exhale as you do a double hammerfist strike (5-8), pause, and then inhale as you do a chest lateral stretch (9-10). Pause, make a semicircle and exhale as you lower the weights (11). Repeat the process for 10 repetitions.

The four chi fung exercises presented in this chapter will give you total fitness, inside and out. The key to success is staying with it and practicing on a daily basis. For the last 10 years, these exercises have helped me stay fit in spite of major health issues, such as diabetes, prostate cancer, an irregular heartbeat, as well as knee and shoulder problems. It is my sincere belief that chi fung exercises as presented in this chapter can help all of us experience wellness and coexist with chronic diseases. Not everyone can do Tae-Bo or high-impact exercises. However, everyone can participate in chi fung exercises because of the RSVP factor. People well into their 90s have benefited from these slow-motion, deep-breathing movements. If stress is the root of all diseases, it makes sense to practice the movements that can relax and slow you up. Chi fung will do just that. In martial arts, the key to success is based on outer and inner skills. Being able to maintain a relaxed focus can give you the winning edge.

CHAPTER EIGHT

DEVELOPING FREE-FIGHTING SKILLS

Free fighting—the ability to express techniques spontaneously without prearrangement and deliberation—is the ultimate stage of development every great fighter seeks to reach. There are basic drills and rules to follow to reach this free-fighting skill level.

One of the best ways to develop free-fighting skills is through shadow fighting. Free fighting is not just a physical phenomenon but also the integration of body, mind, emotion, spirit and chi flow into a single unit, and shadow fighting is an excellent way to integrate them. When the five components of being are in unity, expression becomes free and uninhibited. Shadow fighting gives you, the practitioner, an opportunity to develop these skills without the fear of getting hit by a live opponent or sparring partner. Shadow fighting prepares you for sparring with a live sparring partner by helping you develop muscle memory, a calm mind-set and emotional discipline for free expression.

SHADOW FIGHTING

One of the advantages of shadow fighting is that it challenges you to be innovative and creative. It also challenges you to create a scenario for your opponent. When you can create every imaginable way an invisible opponent can attack, counter and defend against you, you will be prepared for a real opponent. Simulated attacks are one of the basic tools the military uses to prepare troops for combat. Before entering Iraq, the military built simulated villages and towns in the U.S. desert so soldiers would become acclimated to the real battlefield.

As a martial artist, shadow fighting offers the same type of training. In shadow fighting, you must engage your mind to create the various scenarios your opponent can possibly use against you. In other words, the mind plays an important role in developing fighting skills from shadow fighting. The imagination is an integral part of developing spontaneous expression. In traditional karate, kata training was intended for the same purpose. The old masters imagined various attacks and developed a series of movements to defend and counter imaginary opponents. Shadow fighting, as practiced by me, is without structure; it is much like improvisation in many acting classes. It is acting without a script.

In essence, shadow fighting is an improvisational drill.

Study the following photos closely and get a sense of the form and flow. Each movement is a response to the imaginary opponent's action and reaction. Be cognizant of the footwork. In shadow fighting, do not stand in one spot. You always want to move around the room, shifting forward, backward and side to side. Try to punch in sync with the shifting of your feet. Try to avoid separately stepping and punching because everything should be expressed as a single unit. There should be no distinction between attacks, counters and defense. The following photos are an example of how to shadow-fight, but you can create your own combinations and sequences.

SHADOW-FIGHTING DRILL

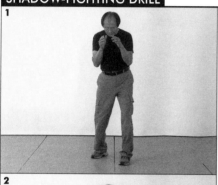

(1) Begin by moving gracefully around the room. Shoot out a left open-hand jab, imagining that you are baiting your opponent to react.

(2) Once your imaginary opponent reacts, step and execute a straight right punch to your imaginary opponent's chin. The stepping and punching should be smooth and simultaneous. All movements should be relaxed and fluid.

(3) The right punch sets you up for a right hook. A hook from the same hand is very effective because the mind is conditioned to expect the follow-up from the other hand.

Continued ▶

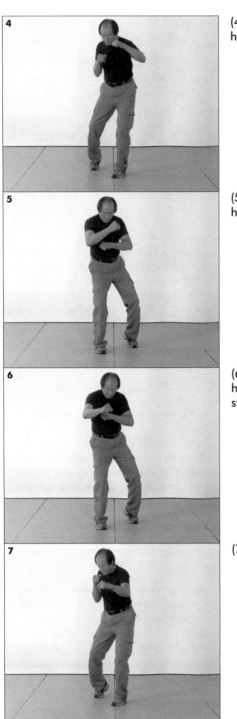

4 (4) From the right hook, execute a left hook.

5 (5) Step forward and execute a reverse hammerfist.

6 (6) As you complete the right reverse hammerfist, prepare to execute a stepping left jab.

7 (7) Execute a left jab.

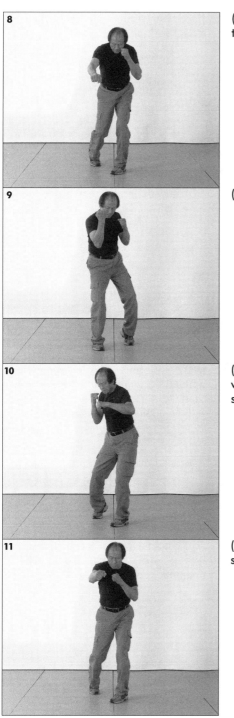

(8) From the left-jab position, prepare to execute a right hammerfist.

(9) Complete the right hammerfist.

(10) From a right hammerfist, step in with a left hook. Stepping and hooking should be simultaneous.

(11) From a left hook, execute a straight right punch.

Continued ▶

12

(12) Follow the straight right with a straight left punch.

13

(13) The straight left punch sets you up for a right body

14

(14) As you sense your imaginary opponent reacting to the body punch, be ready to whip an overhand right punch to the imaginary opponent's jaw.

15

(15) From the previous punch, follow through with a left uppercut to the imaginary opponent's jaw.

16

(16) After the uppercut, slide the right leg backward and execute a straight right punch. Be sure to slide your leg backward and deliver the right punch at the same time. In *chi* punching, the act of sliding the leg back as you punch adds impetus to the penetration of the punch.

17

(17) As you slide back after delivering the straight right, follow through with a straight left punch.

18

(18) Immediately after delivering the straight left punch, drop down and execute a left body jab to set up the next punch.

19

(19) Follow through with a left body jab and transition to a left backhand slap to the imaginary opponent's jaw.

Continued ▶

(20) Complete the left backhand slap. Please note that the slapping strikes are very effective. They sting. They are fast, and if executed correctly with the right emotional touch, you can snap them like a whip. Also, using an open hand can set up other power punches that an ordinary opponent would detect before they're completed. The open hand can help you masquerade your follow-through techniques.

MORE FREE-FIGHTING PRINCIPLES

Shadow fighting is a must if you want to develop free-fighting skills, but there are more principles to apply.

The second principle that needs to be included is staying in the moment. Controlling your thoughts is easier said than done. It is easy to let the mind wander when sparring with an opponent whose single purpose is to score on you. Of course in a street fight, your adversary's main purpose is to destroy you. The risk is much higher and the need to stay in the moment is more urgent. I learned the truth of this principle from getting hit many times during sparring sessions. Whenever a sparring partner scored on me, it was always at the moment when my thoughts were either in the past or in the future. However, when I reminded myself to stay in the moment, I was able to avoid many of the punches and kicks that my sparring partner threw at me.

The third principle is to remember to never pose after throwing a technique. When I would prepare for boxing competitions, I would sometimes get hit by a sparring partner with less experience because I would pose after I punched. That moment of remaining stationary offered my opponent an opportunity to counter. By hitting and moving, you do not remain a stationary target.

The fourth principle is that it is important to hit without getting hit. You need to mentally be alive. What I have learned through the years is that mobility does not mean you should run all over the place unnecessarily and expend a lot of energy, tiring yourself out. Mobility can mean, in chi parlance, "motion in stillness and stillness in motion." In other words, what you need to do is establish a "safe zone" between you and your opponent. That safe zone is approximately 18 inches between you and your opponent. By keeping this imaginary safe zone in mind, you do not let your opponent move into that safe zone. To be able to shift and move at the moment when your opponent attempts to close the gap, you adjust the distance between you and your opponent. In other words, he is forever out of reach but within reach of your attack or counterattack. To make this work, you must be mentally alive; you must be stillness in motion and motion in stillness. When you are standing stationary, you are not really stationary like a lamppost. Rather, your inner structure is in motion while you are standing still. When you are in attack mode, your inner structure is at a stand still. This is the essence of chi fighting versus physical/body martial arts.

The fifth principle is to focus on a single spot. In free sparring, it is common to let the eye wander all over the place. In my own experience, I have realized how easy it is to distract an opponent who is concerned about all four limbs of your body. One of the common questions beginners always ask me is: Where do I look when I am fighting? I tell them that I prefer to look at the spot where the collarbones come together right under the base of the throat. It is from that spot that I can see the entire bodyscape of my opponent. This ability to not be distracted and not let your eyes wander can be further enhanced by standing in front of a mirror and shadow fighting. Put a red patch at the base of your throat and keep your eyes attached to that red patch as you fight your imaginary mirror opponent. By focusing on the patch, you should be able to see your image's hands and feet.

The sixth principle is to keep everything soft and yielding. This principle is extremely effective in defensive fighting. Nothing dissolves and neutralizes an attack quicker than yielding to the attack by going in the direction of the power. Again, the principle of "stillness in motion and motion in stillness" must come into play. This principle is important in that it helps control an undisciplined emotion. It is so easy to become fragmented when there is fear or other factors that impede harmony.

Finally, the seventh principle is to always keep in mind that once you attack, you are like a bullet. The difference between chi fighting and the plain physical approach is much like comparing a bullet to a ramming device. The ramming device breaks through with sheer power, whereas the bullet penetrates, leaving a smaller but much more damaging hole. The ramming device can cause severe external damage, but the bullet can cause deadly internal damage. Such is the difference between the chi approach and the physical approach. The key to making the chi approach work is target accuracy, which in this case are the pressure points on the body. The second factor that makes it work is the ability to remain relaxed and focused.

Keep in mind that the key ingredients for refined proficient martial arts skills is based on the ability to remain relaxed and being able to see the entire landscape.

CHAPTER NINE

BODY LANGUAGE

When I was working as a family counselor at the Catholic Social Services in Stockton, California, in the early 1970s, I realized that body language seldom lies. Couples with marital problems would point fingers at each other. As I listened and watched, the body language was more accurate in telling me what the bottom line was than the verbal explanations. Reading body language can give martial artists an additional advantage in free fighting because they will be able to "read" what their opponent will do next. In order to refine body-language reading skills, martial artists must place emphasis on remaining relaxed and calm, no matter how threatening the situation is. Again, it is the ability to "be still in motion and motion in stillness." After 70 years of martial arts training, I have come to the conclusion that all the elements and all the techniques that are supposed to make a person proficient are ineffective without the ability to remain relaxed and focused. It sounds so simple, yet it is not. It takes a lifetime of training to control and discipline your emotions. "It is so easy to lose it!" as some one said to me recently about an incident of road rage. It has always been my belief that one of the primary goals of martial arts is not just to develop fighting skills but also to train the body, mind, emotions and spirit to respond responsibly to adverse situations. The ability to read a person's body language can increase our communication skills.

The following photos will demonstrate how reading body language can help you intercept, attack, counter and defend against an opponent's attack. The same photos can be used as a metaphor in life. The ability to sense what another person is about to say can help to establish stronger bonds between spouses, friends and foes. These skills have worked for me as a pastor for many years in the churches I serve. It has also helped in my marriage. Knowing and acting on something before it is said can be very impressive in a relationship. In martial arts, it gives the fighter a "one up" on your opponent.

THE INITIAL MOVE NO. 1

The attacker (right) makes a very slight move with his left hand (1). The defender reads the move and counters quickly with a right counter punch (2). To the naked eye, it seems like the defender is initiating the attack. But in essence, the defender has read the opponent's body language and explodes with a right counterpunch.

THE INITIAL MOVE NO. 2

The opponent (right) initiates a right punch. The defender moves to his left at the same time the opponent throws the punch (1-2). The defender taps the opponent's right arm, traps it, and strikes the arm to set up the knockout punch, which is the backfist (3-5).

In chi strikes, setting up the knockout is vital. By striking the nerves on the forearm before hitting the pressure point behind the ear, you can cause an instant knockout no matter how much an opponent can take a punch. In boxing, there are a lot of fighters who can take tremendous punishment. However, with chi strikes and pressure-point targets, the knockouts are deeper and more penetrating. In physical hitting, the knockout comes by shock to the brain. Some boxers are more immune to the power of a punch than others. In chi striking and punching, the striker does not concern himself with whether the opponent has a "glass jaw" or a "sturdy chin." He is more concerned with accuracy and hitting the pressure points. Most pressure points are less than the size of a quarter. The ability to read an opponent's body language can help enhance accuracy in chi strikes and punches.

Reading body language before a leg takedown is very important. Once on the ground, the grappler has a decided advantage unless you, as the defender, are also a skillful grappler. In a self-defense situation in which your attacker may have several allies, it is not wise to defend from a ground position. The ability to read body language is the key to avoid being wrestled to the ground. In the following photos, the defender demonstrates how important it is to act on the opponent's initial move. Reading body language can enhance the timing and accuracy of a counterattack.

THE INITIAL MOVE NO. 3

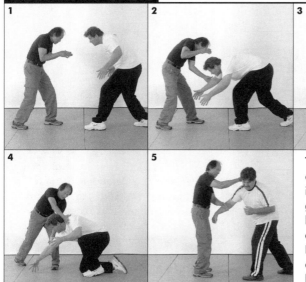

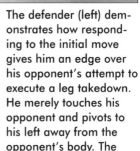

The defender (left) demonstrates how responding to the initial move gives him an edge over his opponent's attempt to execute a leg takedown. He merely touches his opponent and pivots to his left away from the opponent's body. The defender maintains that "safe zone" referred to in Chapter 8. By keeping some distance, the opponent can chop the base of the skull and lay his hand on the opponent to sense his every move. The opponent is too far away to do damage, while the defender is in the attack zone (1-5).

THE INITIAL MOVE NO. 4

1

2

In these two photos, the opponent (left) is contemplating a grappling move. The defender reads the position of the opponent's arms (1). Once the opponent reveals his intention by telegraphing his moves with his eyes, the defender moves to his right and counters with a right punch (2).

THE INITIAL MOVE NO. 5

1

2

3

A skillful kicker can be a lethal enemy. However, if the defender is able to read the kicker's body language and move and strike, he can neutralize the kicker's advantage. When you as an opponent continue to be one step ahead of your attacker, he will always lack timing in his attack. The photos demonstrate how much of a target the kicker presents once you move at the moment of his kicking attack (1-3).

THE INITIAL MOVE NO. 6

Body language is extremely important when facing an adversary armed with a knife. A knife is a very dangerous weapon, even in the hands of an amateur. In order to survive and overwhelm a knife attack, the defender must be extra cautious and keenly aware of the adversary's every move. Timing again is of the essence. So is moving away from the attacking arm. In the photos above, the defender (left) reads the attacker's body language (1). He deflects the knife attack while adhering to the attacker's arm and circling it (2). Then he executes a wrist lock while forcing the point of the knife towards the attacker's throat (3-4).

Body-language skills give the defender a competitive edge regardless of the situation. It is not about quantity of techniques as it is about keen and quiet awareness. When the defender's awareness is so keen and sharp that he can detect the difference between a fake and an intention, he will surely have a decided advantage in any self-defense situation.

The cohesive factor in all of this lies in the ability to remain relaxed and focused. Without the relaxation factor, all the techniques in the world will only be wasted. Emotion is such an overwhelming and dominating factor that you must forever look for ways to harness it and control it so it will not interfere with your focus on the subject at hand.

AFTERWORD

ULTIMATE VICTORY

by Dr. Thomas J. Nardi

Congratulations! You have finished reading about techniques and concepts that will improve your marital arts skills to a great degree. The course of study taught in these pages by grandmaster Leo T. Fong comprises a very complete system for overcoming any opponent you may face.

MIND-SET

The key to mastery is having a relaxed but focused mind-set. The relaxed mind-set has been identified by different names, depending on the particular martial arts. Some arts refer to it as "no mind," while others refer to it as "a mind like water." Regardless of the terminology, the concept is the same: Stay relaxed. A calm body and a calm mind will facilitate the mastery and the application of Fong's techniques.

To master the ideas presented in this book, you obviously need to practice and then practice some more. Repetition of the techniques demonstrated in the photos is essential to imbed them into your muscle memory. "Muscle memory" refers to the body having performed a task so many times that it can be performed without conscious thought or effort. The body just seems to "remember" how to move, without the need for conscious awareness directing the movement.

RELAXED FOCUS

Being relaxed and calm does not mean being limp or listless. To the contrary, the goal is a relaxed focus by which there is minimum tension in the body and few distracting thoughts in the mind. While practicing, scan your body for signs of excessive tension. Tight muscles slow the body and impede reaction time. Relaxed muscles increase the speed with which you can react. As you scan through your body, pause at each muscle group, such as the shoulders, chest and legs, and put your awareness into that area. Do you detect tension? Are you tightening or clenching your muscles? If so, mentally direct your muscles to relax. Breathe slowly and deeply with the intention of relaxing that area of your body. Do not progress to another area until you have relaxed that one area. Take your time! Do not rush through this procedure. And repeat it often during the course of your training.

The body can be trained to be relaxed even while it performs strenuous or explosive movements. So, too, can the mind be trained to stay calm even in the middle of a physical confrontation. I like to use the metaphor of the "eye of the hurricane." The eye of the hurricane is the quiet nucleus of the whirling winds and fury of the storm. Your mind can be an oasis of calm while surrounded by violent activity.

How do you retain a calm mind in the middle of a confrontation? How do you keep the "eye of the hurricane" when you are involved in a self-defense situation? The answer lies, quite literally, within your mind. More specifically, it lies within your thoughts. Psychologically, the thoughts that you entertain determine, to a very large degree, the emotional reaction you experience. It is the mental message you give yourself that determines how you feel.

For example, you're standing across the mat from your opponent in a competition. He is an ugly brute, covered with scars and tattoos. His 20-inch biceps are bigger than your thighs. What thought flashes in your mind? Is it: (a) Oh, no, he'll kill me; (b) I hope my life insurance is paid up; (c) Where's the exit! (d) He's big and ugly, but so what? Being smaller, I can move faster and be more agile.

Obviously, the first three thoughts guarantee you will lose. Your thoughts show you to be defeated before the match even starts. The forth choice is the best. It is the healthiest from a psychological perspective. And it gives you the best mind-set to be able to win.

Monitoring your own thoughts is one of the best ways to achieve a calm, relaxed focus. Challenge the negative thoughts as you become aware of them. Replace them with positive ones. Here are a few examples:

"There's no way I can do this" vs. "It will be a challenge but I can do it."

"It will be catastrophic if I lose" vs. "It may be unfortunate but hardly the end of the world if I lose."

"Wow, he really outscored me" vs. "Even though he scored more points, I can learn from this and use it to correct my weaknesses. I'll do better next time."

Good thinking yields good results. If the results are not good, you need to challenge and change your thoughts.

A QUESTION YOU MUST ASK

As you continue to practice and perfect the techniques and concepts in this book, there is a question you should consider. It is a question Fong had posed to me many years ago. It is a question that I have heard him put to those who have attended his training seminars.

At one such seminar, Fong had taught a group of mixed-martial arts competitors. They were a rugged group with finely muscled bodies and years of ring experience. They prided themselves on their ability to quickly submit anyone who dared to face them.

"How many of you," Fong asked, "can choke out depression? How many of you can tap out anxiety? How many of you can submit ego?"

The seasoned ring veterans looked perplexed. They had mastered their own bodies and those of their opponents. But could they master the adversities of life? They could control an opponent from the mount or guard, but could they control their own ego?

THE REAL OPPONENT

Most people study martial arts to improve their ability to defend themselves. They want to feel safer. They want to feel they can protect themselves from an attacker. For some people, once they have achieved a degree of proficiency in self-defense, they will seek sport competition to test and perfect their skills. They seek to match their skills with opponents who have the same drive to compete and, of course, to win.

But who is the real opponent? Oftentimes, street attacks can be avoided by taking common-sense precautions. Avoidance is indeed better than confrontation. A smart fighter wins by not having to fight. Fights can and should be avoided. Unfortunately, adversity from life itself cannot be as easily avoided. Adversity is indeed the true opponent we must all face.

Here, too, you need to monitor your thoughts in order to control your emotions. Anxiety stems from the thoughts that you will be unable to handle some event, person or situation that is perceived to be threatening. Anxiety-provoking thoughts include a lot of "what ifs." For example: "What if he tackles me?" "What if his front kick is faster?" "What if I can't submit him?" These rhetorical questions are usually followed by some variation of, "It would be horrible!" You need to challenge the "horribleness" of the supposed outcome. You need to learn to distinguish what is truly horrible and what is merely an inconvenience or a temporary setback.

ULTIMATE VICTORY

The ultimate victory is to win a fight without having to fight. Fighting may show who was the stronger competitor physically. Winning without fighting shows who is stronger psychologically.

Fighting to defend your life or protect loved ones is admirable. Fighting to defend your ego is foolish. Fighting to defend your ego announces that your ego or self-esteem was so low, so fragile, that you needed to resort to violence. Fights can usually be avoided if you have a strong sense of self. A strong ego and a healthy self-esteem are not easily threatened by the obnoxious antics of others who have "something to prove." A healthy sense of self announces that you need not "prove" anything; you are secure within yourself.

The skills you will attain by following Fong's instruction will increase your fighting ability. The knowledge that you can defend yourself will hopefully increase your sense of self as well as your sense of personal security. You will be able to be calmly confident of your abilities. With this improved sense of self, you will be able to dispassionately view a possible confrontation. You will be able to defend your life, if necessary, but not respond to harmless threats to your now well-developed self-esteem.

Remember, in the martial arts, as in life, the ultimate victory is always over your own ego. As you complete this book, you are really just beginning. This book is a commencement, a going forward, to further growth and development. It is not the end of your martial art's journey. It is only the beginning.

DR. THOMAS J. NARDI BIOGRAPHY

Dr. Thomas J. Nardi is a licensed psychologist and is certified by the National Register of Health Services Providers in Psychology. He has more than 30 years of experience teaching as a university professor. He is also the director of the New York Center for Eclectic Cognitive Behavior Therapy.

Nardi has had extensive experience practicing and teaching a variety of healing arts, including *shiatsu*, Chinese *tui na*, *qigong*, reflexology, Thai massage and *reiki*. He is board certified as a massage therapist and bodyworker, and as a certified specialist in sports conditioning.

His martial arts journey began at age 13 with the study of Kodokan judo. He eventually achieved black belts and teaching credentials in *jujutsu*, *goju-ryu* karate, *Jalmaani kali silat*, military close-combat self-defense and *tai chi chuan*.

In the early 1970s, Nardi became interested in grandmaster Leo T. Fong's martial art's accomplishments and professional achievements. Nardi was pleased to have found someone with whom he could discuss the deeper spiritual and psychological aspects of the martial arts. The friendship between Nardi and Fong continued to grow over the years. Nardi eagerly absorbed Fong's philosophy and teachings of the physical, spiritual, mental and psychological aspects of *wei kuen do*.

In 1993, the two men co-founded the Total Approach Organization to promote the advanced study of the totality of martial arts, including the combative, psycho-spiritual and healing aspects. Together, they conduct workshops and seminars teaching wei kuen do, modern *escrima* and the healing art of *chi fong*.

In 1980, Koinonia Books published Nardi's *The Mind in the Martial Arts*. This book was one of the first to apply psychological principles and the techniques of cognitive behavior therapy to the martial arts. The theory and techniques in this book became the foundation for Nardi's Neuro-Cognitive Restructuring, which is a powerful method of self-transformation and performance enhancement.

Nardi is also the author and co-author of several books, including *Self-Defense for Women*, *The Hidden Techniques of Goju-Ryu Karate*, *Modern Escrima*, *Dynamic Kali Knife Defense*, *American Combatives* and *Combat Wrestling*. His articles on various aspects of sport psychology, martial arts and combat sports have appeared in leading American and European martial arts magazines. His sport psychology column, Training Talk, appeared in *Martial Arts Training* magazine for more than 15 years and is currently appearing in *The Irish Fighter*.

BRUCE LEE'S FIGHTING METHOD: The Complete Edition

by Bruce Lee and M. Uyehara

Bruce Lee's Fighting Method: The Complete Edition brings the iconic four-volume *Fighting Method* series together into one definitive book. Intended as an instructional document to complement Lee's foundational *Tao of Jeet Kune Do*, this restored and enhanced edition of *Fighting Method* breathes new life into hallowed pages with digitally remastered photography and a painstakingly refurbished interior design for improved instructional clarity. This 492-page hard-bound book also includes 900+ digitally enhanced images, newly discovered photographs from Lee's personal files, a new chapter on the Five Ways of Attack penned by famed first-generation student Ted Wong, and an analytical introduction by Shannon Lee that helps readers contextualize the revisions and upgrades implemented for this special presentation of her father's work. 492 pgs. Size 7" x 10". (ISBN-13: 978-0-89750-170-5)
Book Code 494—Retail $34.95

CHINESE GUNG FU: The Philosophical Art of Self-Defense (Revised and Updated)

by Bruce Lee

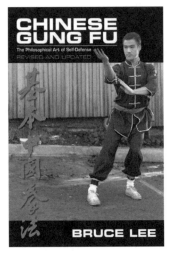

Black Belt Books' new edition of *Chinese Gung Fu: The Philosophical Art of Self-Defense* gives martial arts enthusiasts and collectors exactly what they want: more Bruce Lee. In addition to the master's insightful explanations on *gung fu*, this sleek book features digitally enhanced photography, previously unpublished pictures with Lee's original hand-written notes, a brand-new front and back cover, and introductions by widow Linda Lee Cadwell and daughter Shannon Lee. Fully illustrated. 112 pgs. (ISBN-13: 978-0-89750-112-5)
Book Code 451—Retail $12.95

TAO OF JEET KUNE DO

by Bruce Lee

This is Bruce Lee's treatise on his martial art, *jeet kune do*. This international best-seller includes the philosophy of jeet kune do, mental and physical training, martial qualities, attack and strategy. 208 pgs. Size: 8-1/2" x 11" (ISBN-13: 978-0-89750-048-7)
Book Code 401—Retail $16.95

CHINATOWN JEET KUNE DO: Essential Elements of Bruce Lee's Martial Art

by Tim Tackett and Bob Bremer

Chinatown Jeet Kune Do not only lays out the basic structure and principles of Bruce Lee's art but also reveals some of its most effective and least-known tools. Borrowing the best skills and techniques from a variety of arts, including wing chun kung fu, fencing and boxing, jeet kune do is an eclectic, efficient self-defense system that has revolutionized the martial arts world. Containing detailed photographs and step-by-step instructions on JKD's two basic stances, footwork, striking, kicking, countering and defenses, Chinatown Jeet Kune Do shows the reader how to make JKD work against any opponent.
(ISBN-13: 978-0-89750-163-7)
Book Code 492—Retail $18.95

Philosophy of Fighting: Morals and Motivations of the Modern Warrior

by Keith Vargo

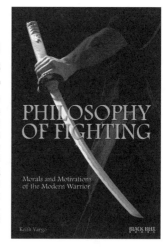

The thoughtful writings of Keith Vargo, the popular author of Black Belt's Way of the Warrior column, are compiled in the Philosophy of Fighting: Morals and Motivations of the Modern Warrior. Comprising a decade's worth of discourses, the book entertains and provokes readers by examining the trends, traditions, cultures, fields and thinkers that shape the martial arts with the watchful eye of a psychologist. By exploring philosophical questions, Philosophy of Fighting encourages readers to actively consider the key elements that define the modern warrior in a contemporary world. 231 pgs.
(ISBN-13: 978-0-89750-174-3) **Book Code 500—Retail $16.95**

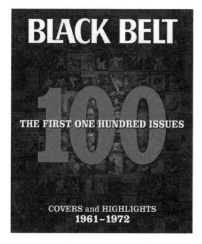

BLACK BELT: The First 100 Issues

Black Belt: The First 100 Issues (Covers and Highlights 1961-1972) celebrates the genesis of one of the longest-running and most influential sports magazines ever in a large-format, soft-cover, color coffee-table book. As a commemorative compilation of Black Belt magazine's industry-defining material, it features the cover art and content highlights of the first 100 issues. Cover photographs and illustrations include such martial arts luminaries as Bruce Lee, Chuck Norris, Mas Oyama, Joe Lewis, Gene LeBell as well as celebrity practitioners like Sean Connery and Toshiro Mifune. 208 pgs. (ISBN-13: 978-0-89750-173-6)
Book Code 499—Retail $34.95

To order, call toll-free: (800) 581-5222 or visit blackbeltmag.com/shop

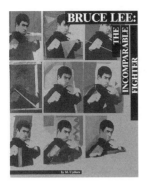

THE INCOMPARABLE FIGHTER
by M. Uyehara

Get to know the true Bruce Lee through the eyes of the author. Pound for pound, he may have been the greatest fighter who ever lived. Read about his good and bad times, his dreams and destiny shattered by his early death. The author, a student of Lee's and one of his best friends, is the co-author of the best-selling *Bruce Lee's Fighting Method* volumes. Fully illustrated.144 pgs. (ISBN-13: 978-0-89750-120-0)
Book Code 461—Retail $19.95

THE LEGENDARY BRUCE LEE
by the Editors of Black Belt

A collection of articles detailing Bruce Lee's rise to fame, including Lee's own famous and controversial essay "Liberate Yourself From Classical Karate." 160 pgs. (ISBN-13: 978-0-89750-106-4)
Book Code 446—Retail $10.95

WING CHUN KUNG FU/JEET KUNE DO:
A Comparison, Vol. 1
by William Cheung and Ted Wong

Bruce Lee's original art (*wing chun*) and the art he developed (*jeet kune do*) are compared by Lee's associates. Includes stances and footwork, hand and leg techniques, tactics and self-defense. Fully illustrated. 192 pgs. (ISBN-13: 978-0-89750-124-8) **Book Code 464—Retail $14.95**

THE BRUCE LEE STORY
by Linda Lee

Here is the complete story of the great martial artist/actor Bruce Lee, told with great personal insight by Linda Lee, including hundreds of photos from Lee's personal albums. 192 pgs. Size: 8-1/4" x 10-1/4" (ISBN-13: 978-0-89750-121-7)
Book Code 460—Retail $19.95

BRUCE LEE'S FIGHTING METHOD:
Basic Training and Self-Defense Techniques
by Ted Wong and Richard Bustillo

Bruce Lee's *jeet kune do*, as explained in the book series *Bruce Lee's Fighting Method*. This video covers the first two volumes, with topics including warm-ups, basic exercises, on-guard position, footwork, power/speed training and self-defense. (Approx. 55 min.) **DVD Code 1029—Retail $29.95**

To order, call toll-free: (800) 581-5222 or visit blackbeltmag.com/shop

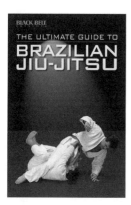

THE ULTIMATE GUIDE TO BRAZILIAN JIU-JITSU

by the Editors of Black Belt

The Ultimate Guide to Brazilian Jiu-Jitsu follows the evolution of this seemingly unstoppable art from an unorthodox interpretation of traditional *jujutsu* to the most dominant position in the grappling world. Spanning two decades of material from the *Black Belt* archives, the book features interviews with Gracie legends, instructions on how to execute the art's brutally efficient techniques and illustrations of iconic BJJ fighters demonstrating essential grappling moves. *The Ultimate Guide to Brazilian Jiu-Jitsu* is the definitive resource on the modern world's most impressive martial art. 191 pgs. (ISBN-13: 978-0-89750-171-2)
Book Code 498—Retail $16.95

STREET FIGHTING APPLICATIONS OF WING CHUN

by William Cheung

For the first time on DVD, grandmaster William Cheung, the longtime friend and *wing chun* training partner of Bruce Lee, recalls some of his most dangerous street fights and deconstructs the techniques he used to survive the encounters. Topics in this three-volume collection include fighting strategies, opponent observation, footwork, controlling from the blind side, edged weapons, disarms, sword drills, close-quarters fighting and much more!

Volume 1: Choy Li Fut Challenge (Approx. 90 min.) **DVD Code 9629—Retail $34.95**

Volume 2: No-Rules Rumble (Approx. 130 min.) **DVD Code 9639—Retail $34.95**

Volume 3: Muay Thai Melee (Approx. 67 min.) **DVD Code 9649—Retail $34.95**

Buy all 3 DVDs for $84.95—Code X167

KUNG FU FOR YOUNG PEOPLE

by Ted Mancuso and Frank Hill

This book for the budding martial artist under 12 presents the history and techniques of kung fu. Fully illustrated by Frank Hill. 96 pgs. (ISBN-13: 978-0-89750-079-1)
Book Code 416—Retail $12.95

A Compilation of Sentimental, Remorseful, Controversial Letters on the Superstar.

DEAR BRUCE LEE

by Ohara Publications Inc.

Read about how Bruce Lee's life, his art and his untimely death affected and influenced his worldwide legion of fans. Learn about his art *jeet kune do* through his personal replies to letters he received in 1967. Illustrated with photos of Lee. 96 pgs. Size: 8-3/8" x 10-7/8" (ISBN-13: 978-0-89750-069-2) **Book Code 407—Retail $15.95**

To order, call toll-free: (800) 581-5222 or visit blackbeltmag.com/shop

THE ULTIMATE GUIDE TO KNIFE COMBAT

by the Editors of Black Belt
More effective than a fist and more accessible than a gun, the knife is the most pragmatic self-defense tool. *The Ultimate Guide to Knife Combat* celebrates this simple, versatile, sometimes controversial weapon with essays and instructional articles written by the world's foremost experts, including Ernest Emerson, Hank Hayes, Jim Wagner and David E. Steele. *The Ultimate Guide to Knife Combat* presents an international cross-section of knife cultures and styles—from the heroic legacy of America's bowie knife to the lethal techniques of the *kukri*-wielding Gurkhas of Nepal—and features essential empty-hand techniques, exercises to improve your fighting skills, and advice on choosing the knife that's right for you. Spanning two decades of material from the *Black Belt* archives, *The Ultimate Guide to Knife Combat* provides everything you need to know about fighting with or against a blade. 312 pgs.
(ISBN-13: 978-0-89750-158-3) **Book Code 487—Retail $16.95**

THE ULTIMATE GUIDE TO STRIKING

by the Editors of Black Belt

The Ultimate Guide to Striking examines striking techniques from various martial arts. Topics include *jeet kune do's* most efficient weapons, modern applications of *isshin-ryu* karate, vital-point attacks for women's self-defense, the vicious spinning backfist of *The Ultimate Fighter's* Shonie Carter, the "combat slap," *tang soo do's* lethal elbow strikes, the mysterious art of *mi zong* kung fu, Jeff Speakman's rapid-fire *kenpo* arsenal and more! Through scores of detailed photos and articles printed in *Black Belt* from 1990 to 2005, *The Ultimate Guide to Striking* provides a vast cultural and technical cross-section on the topic of striking. This collection is sure to be an enlightening and effective addition to any martial artist's training library. 248 pgs.
(ISBN-13: 978-0-89750-154-5) **Book Code 483—Retail $16.95**

THE ULTIMATE GUIDE TO MIXED MARTIAL ARTS

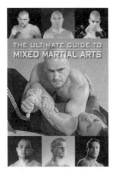

by the Editors of Black Belt
Only one sport has reinforced elbow smashes to the head, flying knees and liver kicks. From MMA's controversial inception to its mainstream acceptance, from the iconic legacy of Rickson Gracie to the freakish knockout power of Chuck Liddell, from the unstoppable determination of Randy Couture to the emergence of tomorrow's champions, *Black Belt* has covered the sport's genesis and evolution. With *The Ultimate Guide to Mixed Martial Arts*, you will leap into the octagon with Chuck Liddell, experience the artery-crushing chokes of Rickson Gracie, devour Randy Couture's prescription for peak performance, master Dan Henderson's winning training methods and suffer the nasty takedowns of UFC bad-boy Tito Ortiz. A compilation of instructional articles and interviews with the industry's greatest champions, *The Ultimate Guide to Mixed Martial Arts* is the definitive resource on the athletes and techniques of the world's most intense and popular new sport. 216 pgs. (ISBN-13: 978-0-89750-159-0)
Book Code 488—Retail $16.95

THE ULTIMATE GUIDE TO GRAPPLING

by the Editors of Black Belt

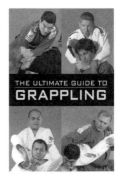

Attention, grapplers! This is the book you've been waiting for. From the arenas of ancient Rome to the mixed-martial arts cages of modern Las Vegas, men have always wrestled for dominance. Ground fighting is the cornerstone of combat, and *The Ultimate Guide to Grappling* pays homage to the art with three decades' worth of instructional essays and interviews collected from the archives of *Black Belt*. With more than 30 articles featuring legends like Mike Swain, John Machado, Gokor Chivichyan, Hayward Nishioka, Renzo Gracie, Bart Vale and B.J. Penn, you'll learn the legacy of Greek *pankration*, reality-based ground techniques for police officers and soldiers, the differences between classical *jujutsu* and submission wrestling, and more! Transform your traditional art into a well-rounded and effective self-defense system today! 232 pgs. (ISBN-13: 978-0-89750-160-6)
Book Code 489—Retail $16.95

To order, call toll-free: (800) 581-5222 or visit blackbeltmag.com/shop